opposing viewpoints ®

SOURCES

male/female roles

1990 annual

David L. Bender, *Publisher*
Bruno Leone, *Executive Editor*
Bonnie Szumski, *Senior Editor*
Janelle Rohr, *Senior Editor*
William Dudley, *Editor*
Robert Anderson, *Editor*
Karin Swisher, *Editor*
Lisa Orr, *Editor*
Tara P. Deal, *Editor*
Carol Wekesser, *Assistant Editor*

greenhaven press, inc.

PO Box 289009
San Diego, CA 92128-9009

© 1990 by Greenhaven Press, Inc.
ISBN: 0-89908-560-1
ISSN: 0897-7372

contents

"In modern societies the family is simply too weak to sustain itself. It needs neighbors and church, friends and extended family—and it needs public policy."

viewpoint 1

Families Deserve Government Support

Robert Bellah, interviewed by Rodney Clapp

Family is a real concern of evangelical Christians. . . . It is a concern of yours as well. At a time of so much social change, how do you define family?

You could adopt a kind of sociological definition and say that the family should be identified with a household, so that whatever persons live together and feel like a family constitute a family.

But my perspective would define family more normatively. You can say sociologically, and certainly theologically, that family essentially involves a man and a woman marrying and living together, in principle in a union lasting a lifetime, and usually bringing children into the world. If you want to call that the traditional family, that's all right with me. Whatever kinds of wider kinship arrangements there may be, this format—a man, a woman, and children—is a widely persistent reality in societies. We haven't discovered any other way of bringing children into the world and socializing them to become responsible adults. Therefore, I would give a certain priority, sociologically and ethically, to the family defined as husband, wife, and children.

The Normative Family

That doesn't mean we have to insist that all other sorts of relating are not family. There are many reasons why one or the other parent may not be in the home. I was raised in a one-parent family because my father died when I was three years old. Obviously, it was hard, but I don't think I didn't have a family because my father died young. There can be a kind of family where people are committed to one another and care about each other without fitting this central, normative definition of family. But recognizing exceptions, I want to reassert the centrality and special dignity of what we call the traditional, or nuclear, family.

How important is family to the commonweal of the nation?

It is essential, but it's quite striking that we pay relatively little attention to that fact. We are one of the very few advanced industrial democracies that has no family policy. Most European societies actually have a family ministry, concerned with all kinds of issues, such as taxation, the regulation of working hours, and legally mandated leave time for childbirth. There are many things public policy can do that will either strengthen or weaken family life.

For instance, our enforcement of child support is extraordinarily lax. In most European societies, that obligation is enforced by the state: you can't just walk away from your kids and not pay for their subsistence. But it is also supplemented by public support; most European societies and Canada have child allowances for everyone. And they are enough to make sure that a child is not going to go hungry. We don't have any such thing in this society.

Of course, there is a considerable concern that if government becomes too involved in these areas, the family's status as an intermediate institution will be compromised or destroyed. How do you respond to that worry?

It's a very legitimate worry. The role of government has to be extremely nuanced and careful. But something like child allowance is a kind of support that doesn't involve any interference. There are no bureaucrats to administer it; it just comes automatically. Most societies in this world have found that's a good thing; it would probably be a good thing for us.

The Role of Public Policy

And then, rather than having activist welfare bureaucracies taking over functions of the family, we need to think about institutional arrangements that will help families care for themselves. Tax laws, and other things that make it appealing for people to stay on welfare, need to be changed so that people can be freed from the welfare bureaucracy.

We don't want the government running our families, but it certainly is the case that in modern societies the family is simply too weak to sustain itself. It needs neighbors and church, friends and extended family—and it needs public policy. The economy is simply too volatile, making the family too vulnerable unless there is a government commitment to sustain enduring family relationships.

How threatened is what you earlier called the traditional or normative family?

For all the troubles—which will probably get worse before they get better—there is such a deep human pull into this kind of relationship that I am not worried for the long run. I don't think we're coming to the end of the family. We are going through a tremendous period of transition and strain, and we haven't got a clear idea of how to get out of it.

"Marriages that endure over time are stronger if there is a fundamental egalitarianism."

Consider the fact that it is no longer possible for most families in America, in either the middle class or the working class, to make it on one salary. With so many working wives, women who are also mothers, an entire form of life that we took to be "normal" in the immediate postwar world, is gone—statistically speaking. That doesn't mean there aren't a lot of families that still have a breadwinner and a homemaker, but they are the minority and their numbers are declining. This places a tremendous strain on everyone in the family. Institutions are not set up to provide a substitute for that woman who is no longer there, the mother who was the moral backbone of our neighborhoods.

Feminist Demands

The other thing that has happened in the same period is a demand for the equality of women. The old situation was in some ways more stable. You could count on the fact that the man was in charge and the woman was important but secondary. In our current society, that situation is no longer to be taken for granted. Husband and wife together are the heads of the family.

Absolute equality is a chimera. No relationship can operate that way. But it certainly isn't necessary for one member of a partnership always to be the dominant member. I think it is possible to work out an understanding of various spheres in which one or the other partner will take leadership. That's much harder than a simple-minded solution that one is always the boss.

And we haven't solved all the strains resulting from the new situation. A few wives earn more than their husbands, and tension can occur. The sheer fact that women don't have to stay in a marriage because they depend on a man makes divorce easier.

Fundamental Egalitarianism

Now the last thing I want to say is that feminism is ruining the family. It is not that we should try to return to the old way, but that we need to resolve these new problems in a way that can sustain strong, enduring commitments between equal partners. We have some marriage research showing that marriages that endure over time are stronger if there is a fundamental egalitarianism, shared decision making. Some patriarchal marriages survive a long time; but if you look just below the surface, the relationship is dead and these people have withdrawn into their separate shells. What we want is survival, stability, and long-lasting commitment; and we want it to be a commitment that's deeply gratifying to both members of the marriage relationship.

Evangelical Christians write and read many criticisms of the forces straining the traditional family. But their accounts usually neglect one factor you discuss: advanced capitalism.

Capitalism is an ambiguous word. Perhaps it's better to speak of "the market economy." Everyone has learned, including the Russians and the Chinese, that the market economy plays a crucial function in the modern world. Any effort to replace the market by a state-controlled command economy creates more problems than it solves. An appreciation of what the market can do, of its creativity and the fact that it has provided the highest standard of living in the world—this is perfectly appropriate for evangelical Christians or for anyone else.

At the same time, if you look at the history of the world in the last 200 years—essentially since a relatively unfettered market economy has become a world economy—you see that it has created a degree of unprecedented social destruction. It undercuts every traditional loyalty, destroys local communities, and makes family life vulnerable.

Some have praised capitalism as a system of creative destruction. Its creativity is seen in the way it tears people from their geographical roots, undermines solidarities, deprives people of what they were trained to do because the job doesn't exist anymore, and it makes them feel they've failed in their lives when they have actually been run over by this inexorable machine. Those human consequences have required social policies to mitigate the destructiveness of the market economy.

Posing the question of communism versus capitalism seems irrelevant. The communist societies are moving towards a greater degree of political openness and market economy. But the noncommunist societies all regulate the market to keep it from becoming even more destructive than it would be naturally. We struggle for a sensible and humane balance.

In what ways does the market economy strain the family?

One way is the sheer pressure of work. Benjamin Spock and T. Barry Brazelton, two of our most famous pediatricians, issued a statement in which they said that, for the sake of the children, the *combined* working hours of husband and wife should be no more than 12 hours a day. That means that if wives are also going to be at work, we need to think about how husbands can take up some of the slack and contribute more in child care, in shopping, in all the things that make a family go.

To me, one of the great things in family life is meals together. It's very hard for many families even to have a meal together because of work schedules and children's activities. But the shared meal is really what you might call a family sacrament. If you're going to have that sacrament, it means somebody's got to help mother—kids, husband—somebody has to help cook and clean up, and that should enrich meals as sacraments because everybody, not just one person, contributes. More reasonable work schedules would help make time for things like family meals. Capitalist industry makes its work schedule solely on the basis of its own efficiency needs, but it is ruthless toward the family.

Consumerism

Consumerism is another effect of the market economy that hinders family life. If you're geared to the notion that the real meaning of life is acquiring various consumer goods, that undercuts the meaning of family life. Some of that consumption is at least ostensibly "for the sake of the family." You want to provide everything you can for your spouse and your children. But if you're communicating to your kids that what really matters is the VCR and the Mercedes-Benz, the children get a strange view of the meaning of life. They're propelled to think of themselves as simply competition machines, set to get the highest grades, get into the best schools, and make the most money.

We need to communicate to our children that the most important things are what we share: family meals, going to church, worshiping God together, family vacations—those are what really count and have intrinsic meaning. . . .

Would you say that our individualism has become so extreme that it strains family ties?

We Americans find ourselves in a poignant double bind. When sociologists ask, "Would you like to spend your life married to one other person?" we find absolutely, consistently in surveys conducted over the last 30 years that something like 90 percent of the respondents say yes. But then we ask, "Do you expect to spend your life with one other person?" and the affirmative answer drops to about half.

This is painful. People want what they think they can't have. This suggests that, though they might not put it into words, they have a problem with individualism. Individualism emphasizes "what's in it for me" and "you don't meet my needs; so, baby, I'm splitting"—attitudes that make it very hard to sustain a lifetime relationship with another person.

Accepting Commitment

So Americans want the freedom of radical individualism, but they don't like the consequences. Perhaps the way to reach those people, whether you're a teacher or a preacher, is to suggest to them that you can't have it both ways. If you really do want a coherent marriage and a coherent community, you can't build your life on the notion that whatever momentarily happens to gratify your needs is what you're going to do. The teacher and preacher can suggest that you can be a strong, self-respecting individual *exactly because* you accept commitments and obligations. And that the *I* and the *we* are not in conflict—that when you have a strong sense of *we*, in this marriage, or in this church, or even in this nation, that enhances rather than weakens you as a person. . . .

What difference does it make that people lack a language to talk about their commitment to things and persons beyond themselves?

We are essentially arguing that many of the people we interviewed are living lives that involve much concern for other people. But each of them in one way or another has problems with how to express that in any way other than language such as "it meets my needs" or "it happens to be my current priority" or "I'm into that."

"For the sake of the children, the combined working hours of husband and wife should be no more than 12 hours a day."

Now, I sense that even if the moral practices are better than the language, the practices will be endangered if we don't know how to explain them. When we have to express everything that's loving and caring and socially responsible in terms of "what it does for me," that begins to undercut the very nature of those practices.

Therefore, it's important to recover a way of speaking that doesn't just immediately, any time any value question is raised, say, "That's just up to individuals and whatever they feel." Of course, many Americans talk that way because they possess the virtue of tolerance. They don't want to reject everybody who isn't exactly like them. But the ability to have a broad, sympathetic understanding of diversity does not require us to give up all objective moral judgment. And we tend, in America, to make that equation: If you accept other people, then you can't come to any conclusions at all about how they're behaving. Our moral practices are being stunted by a constricted moral language.

Robert Bellah teaches sociology at the University of California at Berkeley. He is coauthor of the book Habits of the Heart. *Rodney Clapp writes for* Christianity Today, *a semimonthly evangelical magazine.*

"Whatever their role in compensating for or even softening other types of oppression, families are restrictive."

Families Do Not Deserve Government Support

Stephanie Coontz

The family is one of the hottest new topics for political rhetoric, popular concern and faddish prescriptions. Conservatives attack the women's movement and government regulation for robbing families "of the autonomy that was once theirs"; liberals go back and forth between decrying divorce's "feminization of poverty" and celebrating the new "family pluralism" (occasionally sounding as if single-parent families constitute a wonderful growth experience).

Even some feminists and leftists have been sucked into the debate, contending that they are the real champions of "the family." There is thus a temptation to articulate a family policy, endorsing a particular definition of family and making demands on its behalf for state support.

I want to argue against attempts by leftists to formulate such a "family policy," on two grounds. First, the fundamental assumptions behind such an endeavor direct our attention away from the real crisis of our society, of which the family crisis is only a subset. This is a crisis of social obligation that extends far beyond sexual or familial relations.

Second, most efforts to articulate a family policy rest on a misunderstanding of the historical relation between family privacy and the capitalist state. The very privacy that we often conceptualize in opposition to state intervention is as much a product of capitalist development and ruling-class hegemony as is the modern state itself.

Adversely Affecting Families

Now it is certainly true that the crisis of social obligation and commitment in the United States adversely affects familial relations. The United States has the highest teen pregnancy rates in the world, while ranking 18th in infant mortality; child abuse is high and probably rising; as many as 25 percent of urban newborns have been exposed to drugs in the womb; and even middle-class schools report an extraordinary epidemic of parental neglect.

While many women have benefited from liberalized divorce, escaping abusive or oppressive relationships, others have suffered. Fifty-four percent of single-parent families, almost all of them headed by women, fall below the poverty line. People often talk about the feminization of poverty, since women are more than 60 percent of the poor, but more striking still is the infantalization of poverty. Children have now displaced elders as the age group in America most likely to be poor. One in five U.S. children, almost one in two Black children, lives in poverty.

Legal gains for women in the public sphere have done little to mitigate this situation. Eighty percent of all women workers remain concentrated in just twenty-three of the 200 occupational categories listed in the U.S. census. Despite some gains in middle management and the professions, most women have entered low-paid, sex-stereotyped jobs that pose for them a crisis in childcare: 11 million children under age eleven have no childcare while their parents are at work.

New Kinds of Domination

Developments like these have led some people to wonder if family life was really as oppressive as it seemed in the 1960s and early '70s, or at least to conclude that the reforms and movements of that period may have left many families worse off than before. For many women and children, the break-up of traditional family relations has meant not liberation but new kinds of domination and despair.

Family disruption has been linked to poor school performance, drug abuse and depression among children. Liberalization of repressive legislation and morality has allowed violent anti-female and child pornography to come out into the open. Rising rates

Stephanie Coontz, "The Pitfalls of Policy," *Against the Current*, September/October 1989. Reprinted with permission.

of suicide among teenagers of all classes further contribute to the sense that families need our help rather than our criticism.

It is not surprising, then, that many progressive thinkers have abandoned earlier attacks on the repressive nature of the family. They have begun to try to develop a family policy that can allay popular concerns about the excessive individualism of the modern United States and cut into the new mass base that the right wing seems to have garnered with its "pro-family" rhetoric. Thus the Coalition for Labor Union Women now raises many of its demands for welfare and labor reform in the context of defending the family, while many liberal Democrats espouse programs that put "families first."

"Many problems of modern families are symptoms rather than causes of our social ills."

Efforts of oppressed national minorities to recapture their own history have demonstrated that under some circumstances families can act as a source of resistance to the dominant culture, a means of coping with poverty or preserving distinctive values, an alternative to rampant individualism. Many community organizers, therefore, now prioritize issues and demands that support the maintenance of such families. Some gay and lesbian couples or parents have demanded that their living arrangements be recognized as stable, "normal," and worthy of the label "family." Whatever their differences in defining family, then, a whole new spectrum of groups defines itself as "pro-family."

Leftists should not minimize the damage inflicted by many changes in family norms and relations. We should not ignore the crisis of our nation's children, nor pretend that demands on behalf of children are encompassed by a general feminist program.

To recognize that kinship, continuity and small intimate associations are essential parts of existence for all people, and that children need consistent, personally involved caregivers, however, is not to say that we should organize around a program for defending, revitalizing or even redefining families. Nor does it follow that we should formulate our demands on the state in terms of its services to families.

The Same Old Problems

First of all, many of the problems associated with the so-called family crisis are simply old inequalities in a new guise, more visible now that some of them have appeared in the group normally thought of as middle-class. Capitalism has traditionally distributed poverty unequally within the working class, both outside family channels—through racial and ethnic divisions, occupational rankings, etc.—and within the family. Women and children bore the burdens of poverty just as heavily, if less visibly, within the "traditional" two-parent family as they do in single-parent families today.

The only route to survival for many 19th-century working-class families, for example, was to send their children into the mills and mines. Indeed, the prolonged innocence of 19th-century middle-class children, whose loss is so bemoaned by the right wing, rested on the early adulthood of working children. It depended especially on the young girls whose domestic labor in other people's homes created a "haven" for the development of true motherhood or whose exploitation in sweatshops created the cheap consumer goods that gave middle-class families an elevated standard of living. (Today, too, youth are the core workers of the fast-food industries that make life a little easier for some two-income families.)

Detailed analyses of working-class budgets reveal that married women routinely denied themselves food in order to give the male "breadwinner" enough to get by, while women in every social class have always expanded their paid and unpaid labor, working a "double day," in periods of economic contraction. Divorce is simply a new means of redistributing poverty within the working class from its relatively more powerful members to those made most vulnerable by hierarchies of age and gender.

Second, emphasis on the "feminization" of poverty and on the fact that divorce is now the greatest single (short-term) predictor of poverty for white women and children tends to obscure other kinds of poverty that cannot be explained by family dynamics or dissolution. Indeed, 54 percent of the growth in poverty in the United States since 1979 has taken place in two-parent families.

Women and Minorities

The ethnic group that has experienced the sharpest increase in poverty during the last ten years is the one that census-takers label "Hispanic." Most of the growth in Hispanic poverty is due to the worsening position of married-couple families, whose poverty rate grew by more than one-half from 1978 to 1987.

A feminization-of-poverty or crisis-of-the-family analysis also diverts attention from a process that has been going on among both white women and minority men: increasing polarization between the privileged few, who have the resources to benefit from the dismantling of legal discrimination by competing successfully for management or higher-education jobs, and the majority who are confined to the lowest levels of the economy and never get a shot at equal treatment or affirmative action.

Third, many problems of modern families are symptoms rather than causes of our social ills, and treating the family rather than the cause is at best ineffective, at worse counterproductive. Part of the problem in starting or maintaining families is the deterioration in men's as well as women's economic position.

Young men's real earnings have dropped by almost one-third in the past ten years, young Black men's by almost 50 percent. In 1963, 60 percent of men aged 20-24 earned enough to keep a family of three out of poverty; by 1984 only 42 percent could do so. These are structural problems, not problems caused by divorce or by the "loss of childhood," though they are certainly likely to make divorce, loss of childhood, and failure to pay child support more prevalent.

Declining Wages

The most critical factor affecting family arrangements and their outcomes has been the erosion of those unionized sectors of the economy that traditionally extended a "family wage" to significant portions of the working class. Two-thirds of all contracts negotiated in the past seven years have involved take-backs such as two-tier wage systems or loss of benefits.

Since 1980, steel has shed 40 percent of its work force, the United Auto Workers has lost one-third of its members, textile has been stripped of 25 percent of its unionized labor force and the mineworkers have lost 42 percent of their members. Today only 18 percent of the non-agricultural labor force is unionized, half the percentage of the 1950s.

The fastest growing sector of the economy has been service work, which is only 5 percent unionized (down from 15 percent in 1970); the fastest-growing part of this sector (indeed of the whole economy) is part-time work, which employs women, youths and elders. Demand for cheap female labor is so great that in the 1982 recession, for the first time, male unemployment topped women's.

Such structural factors far outweigh the impact of family rearrangements in affecting the spread and distribution of poverty in the United States today. Even if there had been no changes in the age, race and gender of household heads since 1950, the poverty rate in 1980 would have been only 23 percent lower than it was. This overstates the effect of change in family arrangements by including race and age factors that are not caused by family dissolution, but even so it leaves 77 percent of poverty associated with structural, not familial, factors. Since 1980, a majority of the increase in childhood poverty has occurred in two-parent households.

These problems are not answered by a policy geared to supporting "families." Obviously, one side effect of a social policy that addressed some of these problems would be to make families more viable for those who wish to remain in them. But our most pressing problems are simply not susceptible of resolution through policies directed at families. The family-wage system to which conservatives are so attached—to the extent that it existed at all—relied, James Coleman points out, "on both dependents and incomes being distributed across households."

But recent economic and demographic trends have created "an increasing distribution of income away from households which have children or other dependents." Households without children "ordinarily do not redistribute the household's income to children." Attempts to make them do so through taxes are resented and a lot easier to defeat than a missile appropriation. This has led to a conservative turning inward among many two-parent families, who consistently report to poll-takers their resentment at being taxed to help out what they see as "broken" families or "irresponsible" parents. Interestingly, Johanna Brenner and Nancy Holmstrom have pointed out that the "marriage gap" on questions of social welfare was larger than the gender gap in the 1984 election: Both married men and married women were more likely than single men or women to support Reagan and his programs.

"To the extent that we find healthy families in the modern world, it is when they stretch the notions of brotherhood and sisterhood beyond the confines of blood."

Finally, attempts by the left to capitalize on an understandable but romanticized nostalgia for a more stable personal life represent an abandonment of one of the major insights of the feminist analysis of the 1960s. Whatever their role in compensating for or even softening other types of oppression, families are restrictive. Most family systems, whether extended or nuclear, have been based on the private control of female productive and reproductive powers by the household head. The family may be a necessary means of survival for the working class, but it is one that has been based upon the subordination of women and the highly unequal division of its meager benefits among family members.

Women Take the Burden

Families also tend to substitute the private exercise of social obligation by women—care of the young, the aged, the ill, for example—for public responsibility in this arena. Women as a gender rather than people as a community have been forced to shoulder the social dependencies that are inevitable for all individuals at various stages of life. The fact that liberalized divorce and sexuality have highlighted rather than solved the problems of how to meet social obligations and care for dependents doesn't mean that we should go back to the older family, which denied obligation everywhere else in society by forcibly imposing it on women.

Even the far-flung and flexible kinship systems of oppressed national minorities should not be romanticized, for they often have ambiguous effects. On the one hand, they can be an effective locus of resistance to the dominant culture, but on the other hand, they may repress the individuality of certain members in order to achieve this. Even when they don't do so, their positive role comes not so much from reliance on actual family ties as from their ability to use family language and behavior to hook up with wider networks of interdependence, reciprocity and collective resistance.

In early human societies, kinship was often fictive and seems to have developed originally in order to extend cooperation over time and space. To the extent that we find healthy families in the modern world, it is when they stretch the notions of brotherhood and sisterhood beyond the confines of blood. Families that do not do so may be very close and stable, but as any study of families in organized crime can testify, they can also be exceedingly antisocial.

"Whatever the limits of 1960s feminism, its great contribution to socialist thought lay in its identification of both family and state with patriarchy and repression."

Even aside from the analytical problems in focusing on family protection, what kind of policy would we demand that the state adopt toward families, and what kind of unit would we direct that policy toward? Many liberals favor the *Journal of Home Economics* approach, which defines the family as any unit of intimate and transacting persons who share some resources and commitment to each other over time. As a local Democrat in Washington State puts it, family can be a man and woman, two kids and a dog, or simply two friends living together.

Such a definition, however, represents a capitulation to the idea that families are the only appropriate units for intimacy, resource-sharing and—by implication—state support. Clearly, a family has to be more than one. Yet single households are the fastest growing sector of the population. Should they receive fewer benefits and rights than families?

Besides, a family is also less than something, a way of restricting aid and obligation, setting boundaries. It is safe to predict, given the realities of political power in the United States, that the state will choose a restrictive unit to support or intervene in, however nimbly we choose to define families for ourselves. The state also tends to impose class-biased, sexist and ethnocentric definitions of family norms, putting working-class, minority, or gay individuals at considerable disadvantage in legal disputes about family rights.

Privacy Can Be Dangerous

The pathologies of family life simply cannot allow any concern for "privacy" to override the need for protection of abused family members. A national poll by the *Los Angeles Times* in August 1985 found that 22 percent of Americans had been victims of child abuse, the vast majority of it committed inside families, by relatives. Fifty-five percent of the incidents involved sexual intercourse.

John Demos points to studies showing that abusing families tend to be marked by "constant competition over who will be taken care of." This suggests that abuse is an extension of demands for intimacy, nurturing and individual fulfillment that are part of the 20th-century ideal of family privacy. (Colonial families, without such ideals, did not seem to have such corruptions of them either.)

Colleen McGrath points out that battering occurs "in the most 'private' areas of the house . . . in places that are especially isolated and closed off from outside intervention"; it is the other side of the nurturing intensity that occurs in this "psychological hothouse." In this period of soaring child-abuse and wife-battering cases, any program organized around the sanctity of families is surely unacceptable. . . .

Whatever the limits of 1960s feminism, its great contribution to socialist thought lay in its identification of *both* family and state with patriarchy and repression and its implicit suggestion that neither one can reform the other. Rather, mutual obligation and interdependence must be built into both work relations and personal relations, extending beyond the family and alongside, independent of, the state—including the so-called socialist or workers' states. . . .

Feminists and socialists should be discussing what kinds of demands we can raise that put pressure on the state to help those in need while simultaneously projecting a vision of self-organization and mutual support. Concentration on a family policy can only distract us from that task.

Stephanie Coontz teaches at The Evergreen State College in Olympia, Washington, and is the author of The Social Origins of Private Life: A History of American Families 1600-1900.

"It's official—fathers are no longer the invisible parent."

Fathers Share Equally in Parenting

Roger M. Barkin

It's official—fathers are no longer the invisible parent. Changes in American society have initiated a new family structure. More fathers now are assuming an equal partnership to raise children, an increased involvement that crosses all cultural and socioeconomic classes. Indeed, in many families, fathers have assumed a major role in shared parenting or become the primary care-giver when divorce or death intervenes. These enormous changes in the family present a challenging opportunity that few fathers had in the past.

Historically, men have been considered to possess minimal child-raising skills, a notion that obviously has proven untrue. Stereotyping of our sociocultural and economic environment has led to distinct role identification that is passe. Traditional concepts of parenting derived from our own fathers have changed. In every setting where it has been tested, men quickly acquire the skills and sensitivity necessary for nurturing. Increasingly, elementary and secondary school education is providing children with an earlier understanding of the changing role of men in society. Evolving attitudes toward the balance of family and work have produced a marked rethinking of roles.

Mothers no longer are stereotyped as the only parent raising the children and fathers as the career-minded disciplinarian. Bringing home a paycheck and periodically reading an obligatory bedtime story is not the model for today's fathers.

Now, fathers are involved more intimately in the parenting process. Once banned to the waiting room, fathers participate during childbirth and are present in the delivery room at the cherished moment. Only 25% of fathers attended deliveries in the early 1970's; this has escalated to over 75%.

Fathers continue to be involved in all aspects of nurturing children, whether it is cradling an infant, changing diapers, giving bottles, going shopping, or a variety of other activities on a constant basis. These changes are evident in daily life and even are reflected in advertising messages for infant products—men changing diapers, giving baths, and feeding children. Fathers share car-pooling responsibilities, take children to day care, attend school on parents' day, stay home when someone is sick, and accompany their children to the doctor's office for regular check-ups. Coaching a soccer team, leading a scout troop, and helping with gymnastics or dance are all joint activities. Some fathers may become the primary care-giver, raising children as a single parent or with joint custody.

Improved Relationships

Shared parenting has been shown to improve relationships with children and spouse. Mothers and fathers each contribute in distinct ways to the cognitive development of their children. Mothers tend to stimulate children by talking, demonstrating new toys and activities, and encouraging warmth and affection. Fathers often spend more time playing with their children and are more likely to roughhouse with them and engage in physically stimulating activities such as peek-a-boo and ball toss. Fathers are less verbal, but more tactile, especially with their sons. Interactions with their daughters involve more verbal stimulation—conversations, praise, and compliments. These differences may serve as an early basis of traditional sex-appropriate behavior. Fathers' expectations for daughters probably will evolve with changing values and increasing participation of women in the workplace. Encouraging them to get involved in traditional "male" activities, such as fixing the car, making house repairs, or throwing a football, develops self-confidence and a broader definition of "being female." Fathers should learn to feel at ease when discussing sensitive topics and educate themselves about medical issues unique to children of each gender.

A father's wonderful, positive impact extends beyond intellectual development. Children growing up in households where parenting is a shared concept are more likely to develop solid peer relationships and the ability to confront strange situations. They have more secure self-images and are less apt to stereotype others in future work-related and personal roles.

Changing Roles

The increasing number of women in the workforce has produced changes in the role a father plays. Now, 48% of U.S. women with children under the age of one have jobs, compared with only 33% of this group in 1975. Sixty-three percent of mothers with children four-five years old presently have jobs, up from 45% in 1975.

"Children of working parents actually may become well-adjusted and demonstrate high intellectual abilities."

This increased maternal employment is a result of a greater acceptance of women in the workforce, diminished harassment, and women's escalating interest in developing pursuits and a career independent of home and hearth. The financial reality that two incomes often are required to maintain a desired standard of living is, of course, a dominant factor. In some families where finances are not paramount, the mother actually may not begin a new career or return to work, but she becomes increasingly involved with a community or civic organization as a key volunteer, which leads to significant time commitments outside the home.

Is there an ideal time for mothers to begin a new career or return to work? Fathers now are asking similar questions. There is clearly not one answer. The decision must reflect the children's adjustment and development, financial and personal priorities, employment flexibility, and maternal health. Working parents often worry about missing important moments—like the baby's first step—but evidence suggests that this is not necessarily a problem if spending time with children is valued. They daily can spend an average of four to six hours if this is made a priority during leisure time.

The impact of maternal employment on children has been studied in great depth. The findings have not been uniform, but the impact has been consistent. Infants and young children do not suffer from the absence of a working parent if day care arrangements are high quality and provide significant ongoing social interaction in a positive, productive environment. Attachments to care-givers do not interfere with the primary parent relationship. Children of working parents actually may become well-adjusted and demonstrate high intellectual abilities. The mother-child relationship will remain strong if it constantly is supported, strengthened, and remains a primary focus of family activity.

School-aged daughters of employed mothers tend to have consistently high academic performance. They also tend to develop close relationships with their fathers if they are warm, supportive, and participate actively in parenting. School-aged sons tend to have better social and personality adjustments as well as higher academic achievement if their mothers work outside the home. However, sons of lower socioeconomic families with a working mother may be less admiring of their fathers, perhaps because of the perceived notion of economic failure on their part.

Adolescents benefit when their mothers work. Employed women (or those with significant interests or activities outside the home) usually are happier, more satisfied, and more likely to encourage their children to be independent. Sons tend to demonstrate better social and personal adjustments at school, and daughters tend to be more outgoing, independent, motivated, and better adjusted to their environment. Children of working mothers also are less likely to have stereotyped perceptions of life roles on the basis of being male or female.

The newly evolved role of fathers and the concept of shared parenting have led some corporations to develop paternity-leave policies, but fewer than one percent of eligible men make use of them. Barriers include the financial burden on the family from loss of income and the subtle psychological pressure that defines work as the highest priority for men. Federal legislation has been introduced to guarantee paternity leave with provisions for reinstatement to the same job without loss of seniority and with protection from harassment.

Making Compromises

Families in which both parents work or actively are involved in outside activities must recognize the potential for additional stress. Fathers who share the responsibilities of child-rearing help to minimize this stress, while fulfilling their desire to develop a more significant role in raising their children. This comes from a mutual understanding of the shared nature of bringing up children. When men are supportive of their wives, marital stress decreases and the relationship functions better. Although this is certainly a worthwhile and important goal, it requires commitment and hard work.

Burdens of time and priorities have an impact on the family unit. Indeed, compromises constantly are made. Work schedules often must be altered, when possible, to increase flexibility of hours, vacation, travel time, patterns of delegation, and assumption of responsibilities. Organization is essential to reducing stress and can be achieved by simplifying activities and establishing specific blocks of time for the family. Delegating routine chores to others and even omitting some activities often is helpful. After all, time is ultimately the most precious commodity.

"Parenting should be shared and savored."

With more contemporary models of parenting providing greater choices and opportunities, men are able to share and become better partners in raising their children. By prioritizing time, responsibilities, and commitments, mother and father can enjoy the valuable nurturing experience. Parenting *should* be shared and savored. Children grow up fast. The magic moments of infancy quickly are lost as the independence of childhood and adolescence grows.

Children should be raised on love and quality time. Expectations according to age should be gauged consistently. Communications must be open and honest. In this environment, men will evolve more rapidly into their new expanded role of father, and mothers can enjoy their relationship with their children and husbands even more.

Roger M. Barkin is chairman of the Department of Pediatrics at Rose Medical Center in Denver, Colorado. He is also the author of The Father's Guide: Raising a Healthy Child.

Fathers Do Not Share Equally in Parenting

Arlie Hochschild with Anne Machung

She is not the same woman in each magazine advertisement, but she is the same idea. She has that working-mother look as she strides forward, briefcase in one hand, smiling child in the other. Literally and figuratively, she is moving ahead. Her hair, if long, tosses behind her; if it is short, it sweeps back at the sides, suggesting mobility and progress. There is nothing shy or passive about her. She is confident, active, "liberated." She wears a dark tailored suit, but with a silk bow or colorful frill that says,"I'm really feminine underneath." She has made it in a man's world without sacrificing her femininity. And she has done this on her own. By some personal miracle, this image suggests, she has managed to combine what 150 years of industrialization have split wide apart—child and job, frill and suit, female culture and male.

When I showed a photograph of a supermom like this to the working mothers I talked to in the course of [my] research, many responded with an outright laugh. One daycare worker and mother of two, ages three and five, threw back her head: "Ha! They've got to be *kidding* about her. Look at me, hair a mess, nails jagged, twenty pounds overweight. Mornings, I'm getting my kids dressed, the dog fed, the lunches made, the shopping list done. That lady's got a maid." Even working mothers who did have maids couldn't imagine combining work and family in such a carefree way. "Do you know what a baby *does* to your life, the two o'clock feedings, the four o'clock feedings?" Another mother of two said: "They don't show it, but she's whistling"—she imitated a whistling woman, eyes to the sky—"so she can't hear the din." They envied the apparent ease of the woman with the flying hair, but she didn't remind them of anyone they knew.

The women I interviewed—lawyers, corporate

executives, word processors, garment pattern cutters, daycare workers—and most of their husbands, too—felt differently about some issues: how right it is for a mother of young children to work a full-time job, or how much a husband should be responsible for the home. But they all agreed that it was hard to work two full-time jobs and raise young children.

The Increase in Working Women

How well do couples do it? The more women work outside the home, the more central this question. The number of women in paid work has risen steadily since before the turn of the century, but since 1950 the rise has been staggering. In 1950, 30 percent of American women were in the labor force; in 1986, it was 55 percent. In 1950, 28 percent of married women with children between six and seventeen worked outside the home; in 1986, it had risen to 68 percent. In 1950, 23 percent of married women with children under six worked. By 1986, it had grown to 54 percent. We don't know how many women with children under the age of one worked outside the home in 1950; it was so rare that the Bureau of Labor kept no statistics on it. Today half of such women do. Two-thirds of all mothers are now in the labor force; in fact, more mothers have paid jobs (or are actively looking for one) than non-mothers. Because of this change in women, two-job families now make up 58 percent of all married couples with children.

Since an increasing number of working women have small children, we might expect an increase in part-time work. But actually, 67 percent of the mothers who work have full-time jobs—that is, thirty-five hours or more weekly. That proportion is what it was in 1959.

If more mothers of young children are stepping into full-time jobs outside the home, and if most couples can't afford household help, how much more are fathers doing at home? As I began exploring this question I found many studies on the hours working men and women devote to housework and childcare. One national random sample of 1,243 working parents in forty-four American cities, conducted in 1965-66 by Alexander Szalai and his coworkers, for example, found that working women averaged three hours a day on housework while men averaged 17 minutes; women spent fifty minutes a day of time exclusively with their children; men spent twelve minutes. On the other side of the coin, working fathers watched television an hour longer than their working wives, and slept a half hour longer each night. A comparison of this American sample with eleven other industrial countries in Eastern and Western Europe revealed the same difference between working women and working men in those countries as well. In a 1983 study of white middle-class families in greater Boston, Grace Baruch and R. C. Barnett found that working men married to working women spent only three-quarters of an hour longer each week with their kindergarten-aged children than did men married to housewives.

Effects on Marriage

Szalai's landmark study documented the now familiar but still alarming story of the working woman's "double day," but it left me wondering how men and women actually felt about all this. He and his coworkers studied how people used time, but not, say, how a father felt about his twelve minutes with his child, or how his wife felt about it. Szalai's study revealed the visible surface of what I discovered to be a set of deeply emotional issues: What should a man and woman contribute to the family? How appreciated does each feel? How does each respond to subtle changes in the balance of marital power? How does each develop an unconscious "gender strategy" for coping with the work at home, with marriage, and, indeed, with life itself? These were the underlying issues.

"The women I interviewed seemed to be far more deeply torn between the demands of work and family than were their husbands."

But I began with the measurable issue of time. Adding together the time it takes to do a paid job and to do housework and childcare, I averaged estimates from the major studies on time use done in the 1960s and 1970s, and discovered that women worked roughly fifteen hours longer each week than men. Over a year, they worked an *extra month of twenty-four-hour days a year.* Over a dozen years, it was an extra year of twenty-four-hour days. Most women without children spend much more time than men on

housework; with children, they devote more time to both housework and childcare. Just as there is a wage gap between men and women in the workplace, there is a "leisure gap" between them at home. Most women work one shift at the office or factory and a "second shift" at home.

Studies show that working mothers have higher self-esteem and get less depressed than housewives, but compared to their husbands, they're more tired and get sick more often. In Peggy Thoits's 1985 analysis of two large-scale surveys, each of about a thousand men and women, people were asked how often in the preceding week they'd experienced each of twenty-three symptoms of anxiety (such as dizziness or hallucinations). According to the researchers' criteria, working mothers were more likely than any other group to be "anxious."

In light of these studies, the image of the woman with the flying hair seems like an upbeat "cover" for a grim reality, like those pictures of Soviet tractor drivers smiling radiantly into the distance as they think about the ten-year plan. The Szalai study was conducted in 1965-66. I wanted to know whether the leisure gap he found in 1965 persists, or whether it has disappeared. Since most married couples work two jobs, since more will in the future, since most wives in these couples work the extra month a year, I wanted to understand what the wife's extra month a year meant for each person, and what it does for love and marriage in an age of high divorce.

The Research

With my research associates Anne Machung and Elaine Kaplan, I interviewed fifty couples very intensively, and I observed in a dozen homes. We first began interviewing artisans, students, and professionals in Berkeley, California, in the late 1970s. This was at the height of the women's movement, and many of these couples were earnestly and self-consciously struggling to modernize the ground rules of their marriages. Enjoying flexible job schedules and intense cultural support to do so, many succeeded. Since their circumstances were unusual they became our "comparison group" as we sought other couples more typical of mainstream America. In 1980 we located more typical couples by sending a questionnaire on work and family life to every thirteenth name—from top to bottom—of the personnel roster of a large, urban manufacturing company. At the end of the questionnaire, we asked members of working couples raising children under six and working full-time jobs if they would be willing to talk to us in greater depth. Interviewed from 1980 through 1988, these couples, their neighbors and friends, their children's teachers, daycare workers and baby-sitters, form the heart of this [study]. . . .

The women I interviewed seemed to be far more deeply torn between the demands of work and family than were their husbands. They talked with more animation and at greater length than their husbands about the abiding conflict between them. Busy as they were, women more often brightened at the idea of yet another interviewing session. They felt the second shift was *their* issue and most of their husbands agreed. When I telephoned one husband to arrange an interview with him, explaining that I wanted to ask him about how he managed work and family life, he replied genially, "Oh, this will *really* interest my *wife*."

It was a woman who first proposed to me the metaphor, borrowed from industrial life, of the "second shift." She strongly resisted the *idea* that homemaking was a "shift." Her family was her life and she didn't want it reduced to a job. But as she put it, "You're on duty at work. You come home, and you're on duty. Then you go back to work and you're on duty." After eight hours of adjusting insurance claims, she came home to put on the rice for dinner, care for her children, and wash laundry. Despite herself her home life *felt* like a second shift. That was the real story and that was the real problem.

Men who shared the load at home seemed just as pressed for time as their wives, and as torn between the demands of career and small children. But the majority of men did not share the load at home. Some refused outright. Others refused more passively, often offering a loving shoulder to lean on, an understanding ear as their working wife faced the conflict they both saw as hers. At first it seemed to me that the problem of the second shift was hers. But I came to realize that those husbands who helped very little at home were often indirectly just as deeply affected as their wives by the need to do that work, through the resentment their wives feel toward them, and through their need to steel themselves against that resentment. Evan Holt, a warehouse furniture salesman, did very little housework and played with his four-year-old son, Joey, at his convenience. Juggling the demands of work with family at first seemed a problem for his wife. But Evan himself suffered enormously from the side effects of "her" problem. His wife did the second shift, but she resented it keenly, and half-consciously expressed her frustration and rage by losing interest in sex and becoming overly absorbed with Joey. One way or another, most men I talked with do suffer the severe repercussions of what I think is a transitional phase in American family life.

A Question of Responsibility

One reason women take a deeper interest than men in the problems of juggling work with family life is that even when husbands happily shared the hours of work, their wives felt more *responsible* for home and children. More women kept track of doctors' appointments and arranged for playmates to come over. More mothers than fathers worried about the tail on a child's Halloween costume or a birthday present for a school friend. They were more likely to think about their children while at work and to check in by phone with the baby-sitter.

Partly because of this, more women felt torn between one sense of urgency and another, between the need to soothe a child's fear of being left at daycare, and the need to show the boss she's "serious" at work. More women than men questioned how good they were as parents, or if they did not, they questioned why they weren't questioning it. More often than men, women alternated between living in their ambition and standing apart from it.

As masses of women have moved into the economy, families have been hit by a "speed-up" in work and family life. There is no more time in the day than there was when wives stayed home, but there is twice as much to get done. It is mainly women who absorb this "speed-up." Twenty percent of the men in my study shared housework equally. Seventy percent of men did a substantial amount (less than half but more than a third), and 10 percent did less than a third. Even when couples share more equitably in the work at home, women do two-thirds of the *daily* jobs at home, like cooking and cleaning up—jobs that fix them into a rigid routine. Most women cook dinner and most men change the oil in the family car. But, as one mother pointed out, dinner needs to be prepared every evening around six o'clock, whereas the car oil needs to be changed every six months, any day around that time, any time that day. Women do more childcare than men, and men repair more household appliances. A child needs to be tended daily while the repair of household appliances can often wait "until I have time." Men thus have more control over *when* they make their contributions than women do. They may be very busy with family chores but, like the executive who tells his secretary to "hold my calls," the man has more control over his time. The job of the working mother, like that of the secretary, is usually to "take the calls."

Another reason women may feel more strained than men is that women more often do two things at once—for example, write checks and return phone calls, vacuum and keep an eye on a three-year-old, fold laundry and think out the shopping list. Men more often cook dinner *or* take a child to the park. Indeed, women more often juggle three spheres—job, children, and housework—while most men juggle two—job and children. For women, two activities compete with their time with children, not just one.

Beyond doing more at home, women also devote *proportionately more* of their time at home to housework and proportionately less of it to childcare. Of all the time men spend working at home, more of it goes to childcare. That is, working wives spend relatively more time "mothering the house"; husbands spend more time "mothering" the children. Since most parents prefer to tend to their children than clean house, men do more of what they'd rather do. More men than women take their children on "fun" outings to the park, the zoo, the movies. Women spend more time on maintenance, feeding and bathing children, enjoyable activities to be sure, but often less leisurely or "special" than going to the zoo. Men also do fewer of the "undesirable" household chores: fewer men than women wash toilets and scrub the bathroom. . . .

The exodus of women into the economy has not been accompanied by a cultural understanding of marriage and work that would make this transition smooth. The workforce has changed. Women have changed. But most workplaces have remained inflexible in the face of the family demands of their workers; and at home, most men have yet to really adapt to the changes in women. This strain between the change in women and the absence of change in much else leads me to speak of a "stalled revolution."

"Caring for children is the most important part of the second shift."

A society which did not suffer from this stall would be a society *humanely* adapted to the fact that most women work outside the home. The workplace would allow parents to work part time, to share jobs, to work flexible hours, to take parental leaves to give birth, tend a sick child, or care for a well one. As Delores Hayden has envisioned in *Redesigning the American Dream*, it would include affordable housing closer to places of work, and perhaps community-based meal and laundry services. It would include men whose notion of manhood encouraged them to be active parents and share at home. In contrast, a stalled revolution lacks social arrangements that ease life for working parents, and lacks men who share the second shift. . . .

A Father's Influence

In a time of stalled revolution—when women have gone to work, but the workplace, the culture, and most of all, the men, have not adjusted themselves to this new reality—children can be the victims. Most working mothers are already doing all they can, doing that extra month a year. It is men who can do more. . . .

Caring for children is the most important part of the second shift, and the effects of a man's care or his neglect will show up again and again through time—in the child as a child, in the child as an adult, and probably also in the child's own approach to fatherhood, and in generations of fathers to come. Active fathers are often in reaction against a passive, detached father. But an exceptionally warmhearted

man could light the way still better. In the last forty years, many women have made a historic shift into the economy. Now it is time for a whole generation of men to make a second historic shift—into work at home.

Arlie Hochschild is a sociology professor at the University of California at Berkeley. She is the author of The Managed Heart. *Anne Machung served as research assistant for Hochschild's study on working families, which was published as* The Second Shift.

"I learned . . . that my own pleasure in the children was vital, that my capacity to treasure them should not be taken for granted."

Motherhood Is Fulfilling

Molly Layton

When I was a dreamy little Texas girl roaming the soft hills beside my home, I never thought "too awful long" of becoming a mother. My friend Puddin and I played fashion design and put on elaborate shows—the Months of the Year was a favorite theme—but we avoided dolls. I was a terrible baby sitter, well-meaning but inept. I preferred reading.

Nonetheless, when I was a 23-year-old graduate student and finishing up notes for an oral report on the *Philosophical Investigations* of Wittgenstein, I went into labor. My husband, Charles, and I dropped the paper off at a friend's house so he could present it in my stead at a philosophy seminar. Then we drove through Austin's balmy November twilight to the local hospital where David, six pounds and so-many ounces, was born early the next morning.

It was the ordinariness of becoming a mother that first struck me with a hot blast of wonder. Women had babies all the time, and yet in the great novels I had read, no one ever talked about the experience of becoming a mother, nor about the sticky details of birthing and nursing. As a person accustomed to research, I found even the most practical information hard to come by. This was in 1966, and I had to send off to France for a book about the new Lamaze method of childbirth. Because of the popularity of bottles, even the informal lore of breastfeeding, handed down from older to younger women, had been lost. It seemed I had landed at the center of human life and, surprisingly, found myself alone, engulfed in an inchoate and banal silence. How bewildering that a process as grand and scary and tedious as becoming a mother should be so *unremarkable*, literally not worthy of remark.

I myself was adrift in immaturity, about as unformed and malleable as my own small baby, who, I was now genuinely startled to discover, needed my

Molly Layton, "The Mother Journey," *The Family Therapy Networker,* September/October 1989. Reprinted with permission.

intense concentration. Before he was born, the fetal David was a rosy abstraction in a blithely comfortable pregnancy. I glowed, I thrived, I brushed aside the cautionary tales. Not until I saw *Rosemary's Baby* much later did I consciously recognize the dark side there all along—the baby as parasite, the sinister "other" placed within the soul-self by strange and alien powers, the invasive fetus vanquishing the helpless mother. This is not merely the baby of horror stories and psychotic nightmares: this is the shadow side of symbiosis.

Early Days of Motherhood

Truly the infant David overwhelmed me. In his presence I could neither read nor write. Eventually I abandoned my training in philosophy to study instead this small, willful, and physically beautiful person. I had to push away my books and my thoughts so that I could hear his tiny demands. David was the person who made me pay attention to the world outside myself, to boiled eggs and washed sheets and flirty babies.

In remembering the early days of motherhood, I feel again that first shock of my own responsibility for this tiny, fragile person, the clear and compelling demand that I harden into a self, a definite persona, that I come out of the mists of graduate study. Because we stubbornly identify with the helpless infants, we human beings find it hard to accept the frail and tenuous humanity of the mother. We easily and sentimentally resonate to the emotional nurturance that we as infants need from mothers. Our infant-selves are masters of longing, and masters too in imagining the mother's unlimited strength and unlimited supply of love. The mother soon learns what is required to support the life of her child. Then she just does it. Whatever she thinks the child needs, that's what she does.

Specifically, the mother's motivation arises from her discovery of a terrible truth: she must keep and hold someone who is perilously fragile in a world now suddenly filled with danger. This demand—the demand to preserve—is so clear and so penetrating that it forces even the most philosophical among us to abandon our relativism and shuck off our existential blues.

A New Role

It was the bald inescapability of my new identity that shocked me the most, sometimes making me proud of myself, sometimes guilty and confused, sometimes just exhausted. But of course I had to stay in role: my baby held me as I held him. Until then, I had never been so located in time and space.

The relationship with the baby is startlingly intimate, beginning with the privacy of the nursing relationship and continuing ad nauseam into all the untidy details of baby bodies. There is, of course, excrement in an amazing variety of textures, colors, and odors, all necessarily subject to the intense scrutiny of the mother, a sort of high-priestess of fecal matter. But there is also drool, milky spit, vomit, nose runs, boogers, ear wax, blood, urine—every drop and smear of which someone must wipe away, clean up, and wash off. The mother must develop a kind of hardiness to face the flow of human juices, and a forgiveness too. She learns to say, "It's all right," and comes to accept the body, its impolite realness, its frailty, its pleasures. The sly and secret delight of mothers, if I may speak for all of us, is baby buns—smooth, lusciously curved, actually tauter and tinier than the diaper would have you believe. The baby is such a sensualist that the mother must quickly learn the language of holding and stroking.

By the time Rebecca was born, over three years later, David had slowly trained me into a fairly sociable, level-headed citizen, less likely to drift airily around our tiny apartment like a balloon losing its helium. Consequently, Rebecca and I recognized each other as soon as the nurse handed her to me. Thanks to David, I knew then how to dampen my anxiety in the face of her howls of indignation, and I knew too the companionate pleasures of rocking idly with a soft baby in the empty spaces of the night.

The Constant Self

Sara Ruddick has written of the disorienting experience of caring for a growing baby "whose acts are irregular, unpredictable, often mysterious. . . .In order to understand her child," Ruddick concludes, the mother "must assume the existence of a conscious continuing person whose acts make sense in terms of perceptions and responses to a meaning-filled world." A mother "assumes the priority of personhood over action." The foundation of the special mode of perception which Ruddick calls "maternal thinking," is an unquestioning belief in the continuity of the child-self despite enormous changes and even contradictory phenomena.

The illusion of a constant self is great: one long, loopy afternoon, when David was three years old and Rebecca still growing inside me, I tended my own and my sister's children. Suddenly I was torn open with grief merely watching my young nephew toddle down the hallway stalking the voices of his older cousins and siblings. He wore David's recently cast-off blue suit, one that I had made, and viewed from the back, with the sailor hat on his head, he was for me the two-year-old David come again. The surprise was that I had not known that *that* person was gone until he magically reappeared.

"The mother's rock-bottom interest in fostering the child's growth sets her up for the continual experience of separation."

So there is a bittersweet paradox at the heart of maternal thinking. The mother aches for her child's growth, but the growth is double-stranded with her joy and grief. In the baby's cupholding, the mother thrills at his growing skills—at his intelligence, at his demonstration of his capacity to survive without her. At the same time, she must prepare to leave behind the cozy and intimate warmth of the baby at her breast. The mother's rock-bottom interest in fostering the child's growth sets her up for the continual experience of separation.

But the most extraordinary demand that infant David made of me was the demand for a resolute good humor. It somehow went without saying that anything negative about myself would be bad for my child—if I threw dishes or sank inconsolably depressed on the couch or growled and cursed at the vacuum cleaner, not to mention growling and cursing at David himself. I had always been a shy, mild sort of person, but as a mother I experienced for the first time my own capacity to be a difficult, even toxic and possibly destructive force. I managed daily to be of good cheer, but did not like the feelings that threatened to surface when I was tired or confused.

The first scary hint I ever had of real rage in myself was one long, hot, exhausting summer afternoon when the toddler David would not go down for a nap. After I had tiptoed out of his room for the fourth or fifth time, he cried awake again and to my eternal dismay I found myself struggling with the evil impulse to shake him really hard. To protect David, I did not return at once to his room, and so the two of us cried in frustration, David in his crib and me in the kitchen. Once, years later, I lost my temper with David, and my outrage escalated so rapidly that again I found myself perilously close to harming him, and at the last minute kicked the door instead. The door was cracked forever after, and I never repaired it so that I would never forget. If we lived there still, I would repair the door now, as a ritual of the mending between the two of us.

A Safe and Happy World

But mostly I found myself cheerily, patiently, doggedly pursuing the tedious details of the day, at my worst like some unctuous master of ceremonies for my tiny and captive audience. "Okay," I would announce to a rapt but two-month-old David as we strolled down the supermarket aisle, "let's look for the tomatoes!" At my best I was sweet and low-keyed and optimistic—the kind of sunny outlook that reflected David's demand for someone to instill in him a fundamental trust and interest in life itself. I felt it my duty to point out things: "There's a cow!" "See Daddy?" and even, "Where's David? There he is!" I would talk seductively or pretend to gobble up his foot or I would cover my face with his blanket and peek out at him, until to my amazement he slowly organized his responses, first arching his back, later squirming in delight, finally singing back at me.

This is the sort of stuff people love to hear about mothers, their delight in their children, their boundless energy, their unending fascination with the simple details of little bodies and daily routines. I like to hear it too. But like all simplifications, it has its cost. What is the mother to do with her cynicism, her irony, her urge to throw the dinner plates against the fence posts?

Instead the mother constructs a world that is benign and uncomplicated, as bland and digestible as baby food itself. And as she does, she finds herself turning into the simple shapes and rhythms of living: coming and going, big and little, time for this and time for that, a space for everything. It's a Richard Scarry world, where the happy baker waves hello to the happy mailman, the postal truck is marked "U.S. Mail," the bakery window announces "Bakery," and flowers bloom in the window box. Everything is labeled. I love this world, its industry, its relentless sunshine, its illusory security. Turning the pages of our book, sometimes I needed to believe its truth as much as the toddler on my lap did, feeling always my own longing for a world in which my child could grow up safely. I was saving the stories about automobile accidents and war and horrible diseases for later. . . .

Celebrating the Children

I can actually remember the first time I felt my maternal anxiety lift a little and drift to one side, and I took a good breath. Charles had brought us to Rose River in the Shenandoah Valley to backpack for the first time. Unimpressed, I had trudged along on the hike up, had dutifully organized our site, had worried about animals, had risen with Charles in the night's drizzle to string tarps over our bare sleeping bags. The next day I sat by a rocky creek watching David and

Rebecca and Charles make great Errol Flynn leaps across the boulders above. I should have been afraid for them, but instead I munched a chocolate bar and admired my children's easy grace, their springy legs, their banter with their father. The rain came again, harder, and we left early, hiking down the mountain in a downpour, only my feet dry in new boots, but the kids chirped along like hearty crickets and my heart was luminously happy at the vision of the family I had seen.

I learned from this and other moments that my own pleasure in the children was vital, that my capacity to treasure them should not be taken for granted but had to be cultivated and treasured itself. I later learned a Yiddish word, *naches*, the swelling heart a parent has for a child's accomplishments, an experience we did not label so well in my Anglo-Saxon family. I worried less and made more soup and lived for those moments when we were hanging around the dining room table running through our impressive recall of 101 Hamburger Jokes. To place a vase of feverfew gathered from the backyard in the center of this table was for me a way to celebrate our own gracious capacity to enjoy each other. . . .

"The mother constructs a world that is benign and uncomplicated, as bland and digestible as baby food itself."

Spring, 1988 was Rebecca's last time at home before she too went off to college. That May, during my daily walks along the Wissahickon Creek, I found myself admiring the dogs accompanying their walkers. How nice it would be, I imagined, to get a dog someday. Maybe in the next year. The dog and I would exercise together up and back Forbidden Drive to Valley Green. She would bound along enthusiastically the way young dogs do. I would be the conscientious owner, careful to train the dog thoroughly and consistently—a reader of dog books, a builder of dog runs, a groomer of dog coats.

It was with a sad shock that I realized the true source of these fancies. One day while reading a short story, I heard one character tell her fictional lover, "Pets are only child substitutes." At that moment, I understood that my happy-dog fantasy was a cover for the decidedly bittersweet departure of Rebecca at the end of the month.

Part of the fantasy was clearly to do a better job with the dog than I was sometimes able to do with Rebecca, who, as the young daughter of an overworked doctoral student, had too often bounded off to school with hair that needed cutting and socks that needed matching. But the truth is, I had to admit, I could never focus on haircuts and socks for long. They were not all that interesting. I groomed Rebecca in other ways. When she had a headache, I tranquilized her with hypnosis and together we made the pain shrink and disappear. I taught her how to write with good, blunt Anglo-Saxon words instead of long dopey Latin ones. Driving the long route across the river to her new school, we talked of Carol Gilligan. I fought the dark angel in her that would convince her to hate her own body. And always, I insisted that she take herself seriously.

"Rebecca . . . as the young daughter of an overworked doctoral student, had too often bounded off to school with hair that needed cutting and socks that needed matching."

I walked along Forbidden Drive thinking of all the wise and memorable things I still wanted to teach Rebecca: Travel abroad whenever you can. Learn the names of wildflowers. Watch out for the big trucks and tanks. Talk to your teachers. Did I tell her well enough how afraid I am of nuclear war? My neglect was so vast, it made my teeth ache. But I did not remember to say it all, and we were caught in time's implacable grind. Before us was a slant of light, an open door. *There was no shutting it.* Our life together was measured then in weeks. My physical grief was bound only by the thrill of watching my last child step into the glare of a vast and uneasy world.

Molly Layton is a family therapist and acting vice principal for the Lower School of Germantown Friends School in Philadelphia, Pennsylvania.

Remaining Childless Is Fulfilling

Roberta Joseph

Nobody will ever send me a Mother's Day card—one of those Crayola creations made by dedicated small hands. I will never search my newborn's face for hints of my khaki eyes or my husband's aquamarine ones, or sing a lullaby. No child of mine will ever smile at me, or graduate, or marry. I will leave no heir when I die.

Now that infertility has reached epidemic proportions this is an increasingly familiar litany. But there is a difference in my case: I chose this fate. I have made a conscious decision not to have a child.

There is still time, my gynecologist assures me, to join the ranks of the wannabe "elderly primigravidas" even as I reach my 42nd birthday. I could still enter the company of Bette Midler, Cybill Shepherd, and my own delighted friends, some of whom have endured humiliating, invasive procedures, or paid upwards of $10,000 for the privilege. But finally, with reluctance, regret, and not a little anguish, I have come to realize that motherhood is simply not for me.

Most major life decisions have come easily to me—I picked my profession as a psychoanalyst at age 10. But not this one. I have always been ambivalent about motherhood. I never categorically ruled it out (sterilization would have foreclosed the possibility of changing my mind), but I never felt a longing for children either. My husband knew my doubts when we married. Since I am not the kind of person to leave something so momentous to chance, a child would have to be planned. In my mid-30s, when I was finally in the position to give it serious consideration, I found myself postponing pregnancy every time I contemplated it. I'll try after we get back from Bali, I thought, or next semester when I don't have to teach at 8 a.m.

Pregnancy itself never appealed to me, but I knew I would tolerate it if necessary. The biggest obstacle

turned out to be how I felt about such an enormous upheaval in my life, and the intrusion and interference it represented. On the most overt level, I dreaded the ordeal of moving, reorganizing my complex schedule, interviewing housekeepers. No more midnight suppers, I thought, or spontaneous jaunts, or concert series without elaborate planning, for 20 years. My time would never again be fully my own. My resistance to all the necessary changes and conditions a child would bring always seemed more compelling than any gratification I could anticipate.

I thrive on being able to do what I want when I want unimpeded. I saw that it simply would not be possible to continue to live my way and be a responsible parent—or a happy one. I spent years making my life the way it is, and I knew I wanted to keep it. Despite what the women's magazines say, I couldn't really see a way to have it all.

Being Certain

But I wanted to be as certain as I could be. At 40, just to be sure I wasn't agonizing for nothing, my husband and I were checked medically. The verdict: Conception was problematic but possible. The choice was still mine to make, and I saw that my feelings were no different. Now, two years later, it is increasingly clear to me that I am not moving toward maternity. Deciding to maintain the status quo of one's life is a less dramatic choice than to change it radically, but a profound choice nonetheless, and for me a painfully conscious one.

Probably the hardest thing about making the decision not to have a child is that biology precludes reconsidering it; very soon the opportunity will be lost forever. If I find at 50 that something fundamental is missing from my life because of my choice, I can't fix it. I couldn't even adopt then. In my experience nothing has ever felt as final, as irrevocable, as this. You can get divorced, change professions, or leave town, but not having children

Roberta Joseph, "Deciding Against Motherhood: One's Woman Story," *Utne Reader*, January/February 1990. Originally published in the August 23, 1989 issue of *7 Days* magazine. Reprinted with permission.

takes you down a road where you can see that there's no going back.

Making a will (as I did recently) with no child to leave your possessions to is a graphic reminder of mortality. My life, my world, everything I value ends with me. I will never have as direct an impact on anyone as a parent has on a child; my patients, if I do my job right, go their own way. Without the rationalization or the consolation of a biological legacy, whatever I achieve is solely my responsibility.

"People my age seem obsessed with the accoutrements and activities of parenthood."

Every time I watch the sidewalk parade of Snuglis and strollers I feel like an outsider to the main preoccupation of my generation. People my age seem obsessed with the accoutrements and activities of parenthood, and my life seems radically different from theirs. There are times when I feel painfully alienated from even my dearest friends, who now as parents inhabit a world I do not want to share. They don't appear to be oppressed by its constraints, or they deny or suppress it. They get up early and go to bed early, and of necessity have less time for me.

In my own as well as other people's eyes, my action brands me as different, forces me into a particularly threatening form of nonconformity, which derives not from a wish to rebel but from a realization that my prerequisites for happiness are outside the norm.

Because of me, the course of my husband's life changes as well. He, too, feels a sense of lost possibilities, although he says it is less wrenching. He would have had children if we both wanted them, and acknowledges his own mixed feelings. As a man, his concern is more that this choice is irresponsible or immature than it is unnatural.

Childlessness naturally affects a woman more than a man. A man can eschew fatherhood without any threat to his masculinity, but motherhood has always defined a woman's purpose and value. There is no male equivalent of the word "barren," with its connotations of empty lifelessness.

A Conservative Backlash

More than my personal psychology is involved here. The current baby boom that I am declining to join in part reflects a backlash from the more confident and expansive '70s, when women seemed finally to be disencumbering themselves of sex-role stereotypes. In this more conservative era, an untraditional life once again becomes harder to justify and sustain.

Still, despite feminism and common sense, I find it difficult not to feel defective and ashamed about not wanting to be a mother, or to feel fully feminine just as I am. What real woman voluntarily turns her back on reproduction or does not naturally want to take care of a baby? How can she put her own life first? I struggle to accept as valid and sufficient alternative ways of nurturing outside the literal maternal role—the relationships with my husband, my friends, my students, and the suffering children within my patients. Only slowly do I see that I feel relief that only one of them actually lives with me.

The deciding factor is that my history and personality make me require (for my own well-being) a certain freedom from constraint. Being my own mother's daughter has made this inevitable. I was the focus of her ambition and energy, the bearer of her destiny. She could not consistently tolerate my emotional autonomy. Fundamental needs of mine conflicted with hers, so that along with all the gifts for living that I received from her came an extreme sensitivity to intrusion, virtually instinctive now.

I don't feel—and I spend most of my waking hours helping others realize—that a woman is doomed to repeat her mother's life or her own childhood, or that parents are to blame for one's fate. I also know that family relationships have effects that cannot always be undone. Because of who I am, I must forgo certain experiences to assure that I have what I need most. This means that things others tolerate I do not, that I would be too bothered by constant arrangements and impingements, by the responses demanded by a child, things that would seem less disruptive to someone with a different past.

In Search of Full Acceptance

Many people gain maturity by becoming parents; I hope to achieve it by choosing not to. This demands self-reliance; when there is no one to live through you must seek meaning within yourself. I won't have the excuse of parenthood as a substitute for personal accomplishment. I know everything depends on me. It really does for everybody, but children can permit parents to avoid this awareness for long stretches.

I wish I could say with confidence that all my doubts are resolved and that I live serenely with my choice—or even that I am sure I won't change my mind. Will my house someday feel too terribly quiet, or my interests insufficient? Perhaps full acceptance of this choice is impossible now. It may be only in retrospect that I will finally attain a sense of peace about it and know as much as one ever can that what I did was right for me, that I succeeded in having an empty womb but a full life.

Roberta Joseph is the pseudonym of a psychoanalyst in New York City.

Flexible Work Schedules Benefit Working Families

Ronni Sandroff

When people came to work and said, "We've got automobiles," employers said, "Oh, we've got to build some parking lots." When Americans became diet-conscious, company cafeterias added salad bars. So why, asks Congresswoman Patricia Schroeder, have companies been so slow to accommodate the family needs of the two-career couples who have flooded the work force over the past 15 years?

At the heart of the delay has been the mistaken perception that child care is a women's issue. And that women managers who lobby for such "privileges" as maternity leaves, flexible work hours and subsidized day care don't have the company's finances in mind.

Working Fathers

This perception finally has begun to dissipate, largely because of the number of women in the work force. Close to half of all workers now are female—and about 90 percent of these women expect to have children while employed. Likewise, caring for an elderly parent increasingly is becoming a reality with demands on one's time similar to those of caring for children. Companies that don't have policies to deal with all this simply have their heads in the sand.

And it's not just female employees who are affected by family policies. Today a statement like, "I'm staying with this job because it's close to the house and I can pick up the kids from day care," is nearly as likely to come from Dad as from Mom. In 11 percent of American households, women earn more than their working husbands, and in those families the whole question of child-care responsibility takes on a different coloration. No matter how much the woman is making, her salary usually is essential for keeping the family economy afloat. So working fathers have a vested interest in making it possible for their wives to keep their jobs.

In some cases it's more than lifestyle at stake. Some family-minded men are finding that their career-conscious wives are unwilling to have children unless shared child care is agreed upon beforehand.

That's why the idea of a Mommy Track, which drew so much media attention in 1989, seems out of step with the times. "Today both men and women are saying that they're willing to accept reduced income and slower career growth in order to be more involved with their families," says Max Messmer, chairman of the recruitment firm Robert Half International. "Employers will have to respond with a less rigid work environment. Astute managers will reexamine the 9-to-5 syndrome and experiment with creative work options, such as the Parent Track." The *Parent* Track? A corporate understanding that both sexes—not just women—need and want work flexibility that allows them to arrange their schedules so that not only does the job get done but they also are able to be involved in their children's lives for more than an hour a day. It is an especially attractive concept now, when 9 to 5 often means 8 to 7.

Since dual-income families pose a new challenge to industry, managers must find out what working parents need from their companies, take advantage of government incentives to create model programs, and help their companies move beyond ad hoc solutions to people-friendly policies that extend work flexibility to nonparents who have other personal priorities, such as going back to school or writing a book.

What Do Parents Want?

"When Isabel was born, I told my wife that I would always be the one who came in late or had to leave early because of the baby," says Brooks Clark, who was then a writer at *Sports Illustrated.* He figured that, because he was a man, being Mr. Mom would not have as devastating an effect on his job as the role would have on his wife's. She was a buyer for Brooks

Brothers in New York. But Clark soon realized he was wrong. Writers at *Sports Illustrated* often are expected to work seven-day weeks—something he no longer could do.

So when Whittle Communications tried to convince Clark to relocate to Knoxville, Tennessee, where it's based, part of the recruiting message he heard was, "This is what you need for your family." The lure of a short commute and a family-friendly company did the trick. "My boss has a kid and also puts in some of his extra hours early in the morning rather than working late," he says.

Karen Ramsay Clark found a job in Knoxville as director of planning and distribution for Ira A. Watson Co., a department-store chain in the South. "A smaller, southern company like Watson's turned out to be more flexible than Brooks Brothers," she says. While the move to more accommodating companies has not made the Clarks' family life exactly easy, it has made it manageable. "We each do 70 percent of the child care," jokes Ramsay Clark.

The Clarks are not alone. Nearly 8 out of 10 American women *and* men prefer a job that gives them adequate time for their families, even if it means slower career advancement, according to a survey conducted by Robert Half International. Two-thirds of the 1,000 workers surveyed also said they would be willing to reduce work hours and salaries to gain more free time—a surprising finding in light of the get-ahead mentality supposedly driving American industry.

An increasing number of people also are interested in flexible hours. A 1988 survey at the Du Pont Company found that half of the women and a quarter of the men who use child care have considered switching to an employer that has more flexible work arrangements. "Work and family issues, including child care, parental leave and care for sick children, have become major concerns for an increasing number of male employees," says Du Pont personnel manager Benjamin D. Wilkerson.

The Government's Role

Until very recently, the business community had to cope with the needs of two-career couples pretty much on its own. The government had failed to provide any leadership on the issue, as if unsure whether working mothers were here to stay.

"Every other industrialized country has parental-leave laws," Congresswoman Schroeder points out. "We're the only country where a woman can be fired for having a baby."

And possibly the only country where having a baby creates so much stress. When fathers and mothers in West Germany and Sweden were asked if they were overly stressed from balancing their work and family lives, they seemed surprised at the question and reported little stress, says Ellen Galinsky, co-president of the Families and Work Institute, who did the study

for the National Academy of Sciences. "Even the most macho businessmen declared that people should be multidimensional," Galinsky says. She believes that these attitudes grow out of a culture that is supportive of working parents.

In this country the stress of balancing career and child care is legendary. . . .

Congressman Augustus Hawkins (D, CA) points out that the US is running out of qualified individuals for the work force. "Between now and the year 2000, women and minorities will constitute 85 percent of the new entrants into the labor force," he says. "We can't afford to lose them."

Strong child-care and maternity-leave legislation could be the beginning of a new national policy that truly is profamily and probusiness. . . .

"Nearly 8 out of 10 American women and men prefer a job that gives them adequate time for their families, even if it means slower career advancement."

The immediate task for managers is to get family issues on the company agenda. "The main thing I hear from corporate America is that no one is talking about family issues," says Congresswoman Schroeder. "Though some star quarterbacks of the corporate teams—like Jane Pauley—manage to negotiate individual deals, most workers are scared to death to raise the issue."

Sometimes a minor alteration in work scheduling, or permission to cut back to a four-day week for a while, is all it takes for a family to keep child-care arrangements in gear. In other cases, a change to a post that doesn't require travel, or to assignments that in an emergency can be handled from home, is needed. . . .

The perspective gained may foster the wisdom needed for making the tough decisions that upper management requires, such as holding up production because the O rings on the space shuttle are not safe. Or taking a loss rather than selling sugared water as infants' apple juice. The little detours that people take on the road to success are often the biggest learning experiences of all.

One-track minds don't necessarily lead in the right direction.

Ronni Sandroff is a contributing editor to the monthly magazine Working Woman.

Flexible Work Schedules May Not Benefit Working Families

Amy Saltzman

The good news first: American workers, worn down by the competing demands of career and family, have won an astonishingly speedy victory in their fight for flexibility. A survey of 521 companies released in January 1990 by the Conference Board showed that 90 percent provide part-time work, 50 percent flexitime, 36 percent a four-day, 40-hour workweek and 22 percent job sharing. Just a decade ago, job sharing was unheard of, and a mere 16 percent of companies offered flexitime.

But many pioneering professionals who assumed that a flexible schedule would magically bring their lives under control are now discovering that the challenge is to adjust to this newfound flexibility. Choosing to make work less of a priority means overcoming the insecurities and guilt that come with backing away from responsibilities. It means bashing down the impulse to automatically chase every promotion. For part-timers, it means staving off the certainty that your boss will label you lazy—and the inevitable consequence that you will dutifully try to cram a week's work into half a week's hours. Unless you can outline from the beginning what you realistically can and cannot accomplish, and diplomatically but specifically communicate these limitations to your boss, a nontraditional schedule is destined to compound the complexity of your life rather than ameliorate it, says Louise Rush, a San Francisco consultant who helps companies design family-oriented programs.

Pointless Charade

Pretending that life can somehow go on as usual even though the schedule has changed is ultimately a losing charade. You will inevitably defeat the purpose of your flexible regimen—more time and mental energy for personal pursuits. Although attorney

Valerie Fisher's case load and billable hours were supposedly halved when she changed to a three-day-a-week schedule at the Chicago law firm of Sachnoff & Weaver, Fisher could not halve her expectations of herself. When a partner needed someone to handle a last-minute filing, Fisher jumped right in, as always. She couldn't bear being out of touch on her days off, not knowing if a deadline had been pushed up or a client was looking for her.

"While I was at the zoo with my kids or at the supermarket, I would call my secretary virtually every hour to see if a client needed me," recalls Fisher, 42. Before long, she was spending nearly all of her days off working. She ultimately concluded part-time work was not for her and left to set up a small practice with two other women a few blocks from her suburban Oak Park home. Her full workweek is made up of 9-to-5 days, she controls her own deadlines, and the much-shortened commute means that she is only minutes from home in case her kids need her.

Once you accept that no one can manage the same workload in fewer hours, you have to negotiate an arrangement as early as possible that will let you keep the most satisfying and visible responsibilities of your job and delegate the others. Barbara Garlich, a 30-year-old trainer for Hewitt Associates, a benefits consulting firm in Lincolnshire, Ill., was reluctant to give up her favorite task, training company employes in management and communication skills, when she went on a part-time schedule following the birth of her son. So with her boss's cooperation, she arranged ahead of time to shift some administrative duties, such as handling training contracts with client companies and overseeing support personnel, to her staff of five. Garlich's staff got a chance to flourish in new areas, and she freed herself to excel at the work she cared about most.

Total candor is an absolute must. Unless you and your supervisor agree completely and in advance on your new role, your working relationship will founder. An honest discussion also lets you face the fact that your changed schedule will invariably create problems for your employer, though they may be small; you can offer solutions to show your own good will. A salesman who wants to limit his travel time by shrinking the territory he covers, for example, could volunteer to train another employe to take over the areas he will be giving up.

Avoiding Drudgery

A boss won over by a forthright employe willing to bend within reason is a likely ally later, when your special circumstances need to be handled thoughtfully; no one wants to be the drudge who automatically gets the dullest, least-important assignments. Margaret Allison, an attorney at the same firm that Fisher left, convinced her superiors before she went on a three-day-a-week schedule five years ago that she would be most valuable if given fewer but tougher cases.

She got her way, and it has worked out. "My strategy has been to hook up on a major case and give my all to it but then not take on the next one," she says. Rather than being assigned the kind of low-profile, tedious projects often piled on part-timers, Allison has been able to work on increasingly complex cases and has been promoted to partner. Her schedule, however, could not have worked if she hadn't been willing to bend when crises demanded. No boss will be happy about making scheduling concessions without getting something back in a pinch; the trick is to bend cheerfully but never cave in. When Allison works on a case with a rigid deadline, for example, she gives her home-phone number to clients. When a project needs her immediate attention, she is more than willing to shift her days off. But she asks support staff to field calls so that she's not bothered unnecessarily and gets colleagues to fill in for her when she judges her presence not absolutely required. She gladly returns the favor.

"Asking your boss to reschedule a meeting so you can attend shows a greater commitment to your job than does ducking out midway through a meeting."

Parents eager to spend daylight hours with the kids, but without the career disruption part-time work entails, may assume flexitime is a better choice. Flexitime involves a full-time or nearly full-time workload carried out during nontraditional hours of the day, such as 6:30 a.m. to 2:30 p.m. But Kathleen Christensen, who conducted the Conference Board study, questions whether flexitime can work for managers and professionals who are simply trying to rearrange their already overloaded workweeks around family priorities. You almost certainly will have to delegate some of your responsibilities, she says, to make flexitime feasible. Otherwise, something will give, and it likely will be your sanity.

"Last night, my husband and I folded laundry together at midnight. That's about the extent of our relationship right now," says Mary Pat Baumel, 38, a technical specialist with AT&T who works from 8 a.m. to noon five days a week in her Parsippany, N.J., office and at home during the afternoons. The Baumels have a "tag-team" arrangement: Robert stays with Becky, 3, and Jake, 2, until Baumel gets home and then leaves for his job as an administrator at a local college. His "flexible" workday starts at about 1 p.m. and usually doesn't end until nearly midnight. The couple has kept a direct hand in raising their children without making major career sacrifices. But "we have no time for ourselves or our relationship," says Baumel.

A Different Clock

Both flexitimers and part-timers will undoubtedly have to remind their colleagues and superiors frequently that they answer to a different clock. Most managers are unlikely to set meetings and arrange conference calls with your schedule in mind. But asking your boss to reschedule a meeting so you can attend shows a greater commitment to your job than does ducking out midway through a meeting to pick up your child at day care or missing the meeting altogether. "When someone drops a project on my desk and says they need it immediately, I no longer just nod my head and say 'sure,' " says Katie Rhoades, 36, an attorney for U.S. Sprint in Kansas City who shifted to a three-day-a-week schedule 15 months ago following the birth of her second child. "You have to learn to say to your boss or client that you won't be able to get that case to them until next week because you work part-time and need to be home with your kids." Rhoades is still learning how to ask such questions as "Why is that memo a priority?" and "Do you really need that by tomorrow at 4:30, or can it wait until next Monday?"

Making it clear that you have a life beyond work is not as risky as it sounds. The more you respect your boss's need to stay informed and to coordinate the whole team's work, the more he or she will respect your efforts to lead a life tilted in a slightly different direction. Liberating yourself from work doesn't happen automatically. It takes work.

Amy Saltzman is an associate editor for the weekly newsmagazine U.S. News & World Report.

Comparable Worth Is Beneficial

Sara M. Evans and Barbara J. Nelson

On September 30, 1983, the Minneapolis City Council unanimously declared its intention to develop a new comparable worth wage policy in response to labor and feminist pressures for wage justice in public employment. A twenty-four-member Advisory Committee on Pay Equity, composed largely of elected officials and union representatives from five salary-setting jurisdictions (the city itself; the Minneapolis Park, Library, and School Boards; and the Minneapolis Community Development Agency), accepted its charge "to review the existing classification system, identify patterns that indicate a lack of balance of 'job value' between male-dominated and female-dominated job classes, and recommend a program to resolve any inequities." In other words, they adopted a comparable worth policy with the goal of eradicating sex-based wage discrimination. In the midst of their deliberations, in April 1984, the state of Minnesota passed a law requiring all political subdivisions within the state to adopt a similar policy. By August the Minneapolis Advisory Committee unanimously proposed that the city implement a plan to raise the wages of the lowest-paid female-dominated jobs in city government. But the unanimity both on the Council and in the Advisory Committee masked deep disagreements about the meaning of comparable worth in practice. . . .

Salary Disparities

What is at stake in the comparable worth movement? At the very basic level, the stakes are the interpretation of the wage and earnings gaps between women and men, and minorities and whites. Women working full-time earn, in the aggregate, up to 33% less than men working full-time; and full-time minority workers earn up to 25% less than full-time white workers. Why does this occur?

At the more general level the stakes are about the social construction of causation. How much of our destinies do we control as individuals and how much is the result of large social forces as they play themselves out in our lives and through our choices? As an issue, comparable worth encompasses not only deep divisions of opinion about what workers should be paid (and thus how they will live) but also about how society will *know* what workers should be paid (and thus how society justifies the payment decision).

Earnings Differentials

The current comparable worth movement began in the 1970s with the growing recognition that, largely because of occupational segregation by gender, women working full-time, year-round received roughly two-thirds of men's full-time, year round earnings. When arrayed by race and ethnicity as well as gender, the earnings differentials gave further credence to the widespread feeling that the economic deck was stacked against people of color and women. In 1980, as the comparable worth movement became more prominent nationwide, the median earnings of white women employed full-time, year-round averaged 59.3% of the earnings of white men, and Black and Hispanic women received, respectively, 55.3% and 40.1% of white men's earnings. Black men earned 70.4% and Hispanic men earned 69.4% of white men's earnings. By 1986, the equivalent figures for women showed some slow but encouraging gains, with white women earning 64.2%, Black women 56.2%, and Hispanic women 53.3% of white men's earnings. Black men's relative earnings increased very slightly to 70.5% of white men's earnings while Hispanic men's earnings decreased slightly to 63.9%.

Recently there has been a great deal of confusion over whether the wage gap between men and women has decreased rapidly toward the end of the decade of the eighties. In 1987, the Bureau of the Census published a report showing that the *hourly* wage gap had closed to 70%, which looked like a dramatic change when compared to the 59% with which many people were familiar. This early figure of 59% referred to the gender comparison of all median full-time, year-round wages. In 1986, the same comparison of all women's to men's median full-time, year-round wages shows that women earned 65.0% of what men earned. Hourly wage comparisons tend to obscure the fact that women work fewer hours than men, both by choice and because of the unavailability of full-time work. Yearly comparisons tend to obscure the fact that managerial and professional workers, mostly men, tend to work a longer number of hours in their full-time week than do workers with other kinds of jobs.

The trends in the relationships between the earnings of men and women and whites and minorities are also important to an understanding of comparable worth. After the Korean War, white women's earnings first declined and then held steady against white men's earnings. Minority women's earnings made gains against white men's earnings, making minority and white women's earnings more similar. Minority men's earnings made big advances, coming 40% closer to white men's earnings in the period between 1955 and 1975. As the decade of the 1970s closed, however, the distance between minority men's earnings and white men's earnings began to grow larger again, in part because of the loss of manufacturing jobs that had employed a relatively high proportion of minority men. . . .

Other Factors That Separate Workers

These earnings differentials do not, of course, tell the full story of the racial, ethnic, and gender variations in economic conditions. A more complete picture of the relative economic position of various groups includes information about employment, governmental transfers, wealth, and family composition. Blacks and Hispanics are, respectively, 2.4 and 1.7 times as likely to be unemployed as are whites, and the figures are much worse for Black and Hispanic teenagers. Individuals without jobs, regardless of the cause, are likely to receive some sort of transfer payment, such as Social Security or AFDC [Aid to Families with Dependent Children]. In 1985, 62 million adults received at least one kind of transfer. Almost 55% of recipients were women, 12% were Black, and 5% were Hispanic. White men received the most money in transfers, averaging $6,475 per year compared to the $3,474 transferred to Black women.

The race, ethnicity, and gender breakdown for wealth is even more stark. As defined by the Census Bureau, wealth equals the ownership of savings, housing, automobiles, stocks and similar items, minus debts. In 1984, the median net worth of all white households was $39,135; of all Hispanic households it was $4,912; and of all Black households it was $3,397.

White households had almost twelve times the wealth of Black households. The median net worth of white and Black female-headed households showed an even more extreme relationship. The median net worth of white female-headed households was $22,500 compared to $700 for Black female-headed households, a ratio of 32 to 1. These last figures indicate a general pattern: households headed by a woman alone are more financially precarious than two-adult households, especially for minorities.

"In 1985, 62 million adults received at least one kind of transfer. Almost 55% of recipients were women."

While not the whole story, earnings differentials do provide a powerful message in helping many groups understand and organize around their economic status. But earnings ratios do not refer to wage differences in jobs of equal value as defined by a comparable worth analysis, although there is occasional confusion over this issue. Rather, a great many factors explicitly *not* related to equivalent jobs contribute to the earnings ratios. From the perspective of the worker, men and women and whites and minorities often have different schooling, job skills, and work histories. From the perspective of the economy, men and women often hold different jobs. Occupational segregation is the watchword of most workers' job experience. According to 1980 census data, women, regardless of race or ethnicity, were likely to work in occupations that were two-thirds filled by women, and men were likely to work in jobs whose incumbents ranged from 69% to 79% male, the exact percentages depending on their race or ethnicity.

Another way to think about occupational segregation is to move from the census figures, which describe the national composition of an occupation, by gender, race, and ethnicity, to figures about individual firms or jurisdictions, which describe the gender, race, and ethnic composition of specific occupations within that firm. In a study of gender segregation in 400 work organizations in California, James N. Baron and William T. Bielby found that "over 59% were *perfectly* segregated by sex—that is, workers of one sex were either excluded entirely or were concentrated in job titles filled exclusively by the same sex." Baron and Bielby report that the kinds of industries underrepresented or excluded from their study (insurance, trucking, construction, and retail trade) are likely to be *more* sex-segregated than the organizations included; thus they probably understate their findings about the percentage of perfectly sex-segregated occupations within individual workplaces.

Occupational segregation is directly associated with

gender, race, and ethnic differentials in overall earnings. As the proportion of women or minority members in an occupation increases, wages decrease. An analysis of the expanded occupational codes of the 1970 census showed that for every additional 1% of women in an occupation, yearly salary declined $42, making an all-female job average about $4,000 less per year than an all-male job. This is not a comparable worth analysis, however, but was instead a study of the aggregate income effects of all-female occupations, regardless of the skill level, education, or working conditions associated with the job. An "over-concentration" of minorities in an occupation can have a similar effect. An analysis of employees working for the state of New York in 1982 showed that occupations where Blacks or Hispanics were at least 40% more prevalent than in the state's overall labor force appeared to be underpaid by 1.59 salary grades (roughly $7,950) when compared in a comparable worth job content analysis to occupations predominantly held by white men.

Occupational segregation is not the only structural characteristic affecting gender, race, and ethnic patterns in wages. Additionally, white women and minorities tend to be employed by smaller firms and in less robust sectors of the economy than do white men, and smaller firms and less robust sectors pay lower wages. In addition, whatever the occupation, women, most notably women of color, tend to be lower-paid incumbents within it as well. It was all these differences, but especially the fact that women and men often hold different jobs where equal pay for equal work would not apply, that led to the comparable worth approach. . . .

Transformative Possibilities

When measured against the egalitarian vision of economic justice for women and minorities that underlies the passion of most advocates, the concrete achievements of comparable worth in practice often fall short. Yet this may be an improper measure, fated to label any nonutopian outcome as a failure. For example, advocates like Alice Kessler-Harris argue that comparable worth offers a fundamental revaluing of women and their work. Yet the use of preexisting methods of job evaluation by most jurisdictions implementing a comparable worth policy fails to meet this standard. Rather, it simply applies to women's jobs the *same* values and criteria that have been devised to rate traditionally male jobs. In addition, the potential for changed consciousness and cultural values is muted when unions and managers believe that the success of the policy requires a low-key approach in order not to arouse division and hostility. In Minnesota this meant that 45% of employees who actually received comparable worth raises were unaware of that fact!

Similarly, the materially transformative possibility of comparable worth lies in its redistributive nature,

its capacity to rearrange the wage bill, giving women and minorities a greater share. Yet the forces arrayed against any wholly or partially redistributive policy are great. Because redistributive policies *transfer* valued resources, establishing what are often viewed by participants as real long-term winners and losers, politicians are pressured to reconfigure policies in a more distributive manner, where a greater number of people benefit, but often without targeting those most in need. If *additional* monies can be made available, as appeared to be the case at the state level in Minnesota, then even a distributive policy can result in substantial gains for targeted classes. But in other cases a combination of pay-for-points and a series of cost-containment measures have clearly reduced the impact of comparable worth on the incomes of women and minorities.

"When measured against the predictions of opponents, comparable worth in Minnesota and elsewhere has not led to economic dislocations."

Nevertheless, in Minnesota comparable worth has provided resources that significantly increase the capacity for autonomy and independence of women and minorities at the lowest end of the pay scale. The additional income generated by pay equity increments in Minnesota state and local jurisdictions substantially increased the incomes of clerical and health care workers whose earnings had been close to the poverty line wage.

As a reform rooted in union, civil rights, and feminist activism, comparable worth might also be seen as an important source of strength for social movements for economic justice. Some unions have found the *demand* for comparable worth to be a highly effective organizing tool. As numerous strikes and grass-roots efforts demonstrate, mobilization around this issue can be a democratic and empowering experience for women and minorities who rethink the value of their own work and challenge the hierarchy of values enshrined in the wage scale. Yet effective political advocacy has tended to remain in the hands of a relatively small political elite, and implementation appears highly subject to technocratic control. If in the most successful examples women are likely to receive increased wages with little knowledge about where they came from or why, their economic independence may be enhanced but their sense of group solidarity will not.

Comparable Worth in Context

When measured against the predictions of opponents, comparable worth in Minnesota and elsewhere has not led to economic dislocations in the form either of significant disemployment effects or of exorbitant and inflationary growth in the total wage bill. In addition, as the state of Minnesota illustrates, comparable worth can be instituted with minimal disruption in large government (or corporate) bureaucracies which have professionalized their personnel functions and pay practices. Wherever there is a job evaluation system in place, the techniques for estimating inequities between male-, female-, and minority-dominated job classes are well established and simple. A second method that also serves to shift wages quickly and simply toward the lowest-paid women and minorities (but is closer to a solidarity wage than to comparable worth) is exemplified by the decisions of New Mexico and New Jersey to raise the wages of their lowest-paid workers *prior* to a comparable worth study. In either case there are clear advantages to separating comparable worth from the processes of reclassification and job evaluation, even though the results will remain problematic for proponents concerned about biases within job evaluation systems. Indeed, such a separation appears to be the only way to maintain a clear focus on remedying the historically low wages of women and minorities and to avoid giving primacy to technocratic concerns.

A Procedural Reform

At the same time, comparable worth cannot bear the full weight of proponents' hopes for democratic change and wage justice. Clarity about what comparable worth as a technocratic reform can and does achieve can place it in its proper context as part of a broader strategy. What appear to be weaknesses, when measured against proponents' values, obtain only when comparable worth is discussed in isolation, as a single issue. Instead, comparable worth must be seen as a long-term strategy linked to a variety of other concerns. Comparable worth is a *procedural* reform—not the same as creating new individual rights and leaving individuals to enforce them in the courts. Like environmental protection, where one can never stop testing air quality regardless of specific victories, comparable worth will require constant vigilance. If it reinforces hierarchy, activists must consider other, simultaneous ways to press for participation and power. If it is subject to other agendas, proponents must understand the implications of those agendas and oppose or ally with them consciously. If comparable worth legislation strengthens the hands of public managers, then organizing strategies that win comparable worth settlements directly through collective bargaining may offer a different set of possibilities. And all of these efforts will be enhanced if technical reforms can be described with a vocabulary that makes explicit the implicit claims to full citizenship and community participation.

Comparable worth may never provide the same satisfaction of broad mobilization that other issues, such as the ERA [Equal Rights Amendment], do. The tendency towards elite domination (indeed the necessity for that once an initial legislative or collective bargaining victory has been won) and the complexities of implementation make that difficult. Key leaders and spokespeople frequently are union men who must also maintain credibility with their male constituents. This advantages comparable worth as a coalition-building vehicle but removes it from the intense sociability of female-dominated and -defined social movements. The need for vigilance beyond initial victories, however, further clarifies the importance of linking comparable worth to a broad agenda for democracy and for wage justice.

"The need for vigilance beyond initial victories, however, further clarifies the importance of linking comparable worth to a broad agenda for democracy and for wage justice."

Comparable worth policies will remain on the political agenda for the foreseeable future. A process has been set in motion in many public jurisdictions as well as private corporations (though the latter are unlikely to admit to it), and that process will continue to bear fruit. By August 1987, 20 states and 166 localities (outside of Minnesota) had implemented comparable worth and 26 additional states were in the earlier stages of action. Successful implementation in many locations, including Minnesota, provides models and spurs to further actions. And organizations of working women, including some of the fastest-growing unions as well as professional associations of nurses and librarians, will keep up a lively grass-roots pressure. Subsequent reform agendas will probably incorporate the broader understanding of wage discrimination introduced by comparable worth. And in a world in which women and men share productive work in the labor force in increasingly similar numbers, the pressure for wage justice will not abate.

Sara M. Evans is professor of history at the University of Minnesota in Minneapolis and directs the University's Center for Advanced Feminist Studies. Barbara J. Nelson is professor at the Hubert H. Humphrey Institute of Public Affairs at the University of Minnesota. She also codirects the University's Center on Women and Public Policy.

"Comparable worth is not the appropriate remedy."

Comparable Worth Is Harmful

Ellen Frankel Paul

Both the comparable worth opponents and the judges who have been reluctant to read a comparable worth remedy into Title VII base their opposition to the concept essentially on economic grounds. The critics argue that imposing comparable worth would have these deleterious economic consequences: it would be far too costly; it would cause economic disruption in the form of inflation, unemployment, and an inability to compete on international markets; and, more generally, it would undermine our free-market system.

The case the opponents make against comparable worth is *prima facie* quite persuasive, and the question then becomes: Can the comparable worth advocates surmount that case by rebutting the essential charges? After a careful examination of the arguments of both sides, I conclude that they cannot. While I am sympathetic to the goals that have prompted many people to support comparable worth—women's equality in the work place and a society free of invidious discrimination—comparable worth is not the appropriate remedy. . . .

Comparable Worth and Intrinsic Value

When the critics charge that comparable worth depends on a notion of intrinsic value that can be measured on an objective scale, they have identified a fundamental misconception that underpins the case for imposing comparable worth. . . .

What comparable worth's proponents are searching for is some identifiable, objective qualities that are transferable from job to job and that everyone could, at least theoretically, agree upon. But are they not searching in vain? The perpetual squabbles among evaluators performing studies in the states, the instructions of consultants to the evaluation committees that they should go with their gut

instincts in assessing points, and the reevaluations that go on once the scores have been assembled are empirical evidence of a problem that really lies on the theoretical level.

If there is no intrinsic value to a job, then it cannot be measured. Let us look at the wage-setting process as it unfolds in the market to see what the price of labor means, if it does not mean a measurement of intrinsic value.

A job has value to someone who creates it and is willing to pay someone to do it. The price of that job is set in the labor market, which is nothing more than an arena for satisfying the demands for labor of various sorts by numerous employers. What an employer is willing to pay for the type of labor he needs depends on his assessment of what that labor can contribute to the ultimate product and what price he thinks those products will command in the market. The labor market is an impersonal process. In most cases, employers and potential employees do not know each other before the process is begun. It is impersonal in another way, also. No individual employer can exercise much influence over the price of labor of the kind he needs. Only in the rarest of cases, where no alternative employers are available to willing workers, will any one employer have much of an impact on the overall job market. Such influence characterizes centrally planned, government-owned economies much more than it does market economies. To the extent that markets are distorted by government-imposed monopolies or cartels, the actual market departs from the theoretical one.

Worker and Employer Decisions

The supporters of comparable worth consider this view of the market naive. Rather, they say, markets are dominated by monopolies that dictate wages to workers who by-and-large have no other options. The problem with this argument is that it is simply not true that the labor market in the United States is largely dominated by monopolies. What has characterized capitalist economies since the Industrial Revolution is precisely the options that workers have, the fluidity of labor markets, and the ever-changing possibilities the market creates. Unlike the Middle Ages, where workers' options were essentially limited to following the paternal occupation and where class status was very nearly immutable, capitalism presents workers with a plethora of options.

Indeed, this kaleidoscopic choice is precisely the aspect of capitalism to which its early opponents, both of the socialist and patriarchal variety, most vehemently objected. Where monopolies do exist, they are usually the result of governmental interference, for example, by grants of monopoly, and not by the action of the marketplace. While temporary monopolies may arise in a free market, they tend not to last, as upstart companies and their new technology eventually upset the staid ''monopolists.''

To return to our description of the labor market, if an employer, through discriminatory motivation or any other reason, wishes to pay less than the prevailing wage for a certain kind of labor, one of three things will normally happen. He will get no takers. He will get fewer takers than he needs. Or the quality of the applicant pool will be lower than the job requires. Conversely, if he wishes to pay more, he will get many applicants and some of them will be of higher quality than normal in that job classification.

In the former case, the employer jeopardizes his business by presumably making his products less marketable and his operation less efficient; in the latter case, the employer may benefit his business if his more skilled employees produce more products or a better product that the consumers are willing to pay a higher price to acquire. The consumer, however, may not be willing, and then the business would be jeopardized.

"If jobs have no intrinsic worth, then the comparable worth position has been severely wounded, for it bases its case on precisely such an assumption."

Thus, employers are, in the normal case, pretty much tied to paying prevailing market wages. Those employers who discriminate for irrelevant reasons—like race, sex, religion—put themselves at a competitive disadvantage by restricting the pool of labor from which they can select workers. If discrimination against blacks or women, for example, were prevalent in the society, the price of such labor would be lower than for comparable labor provided by members of other groups. Those employers willing to hire the despised will benefit from lower prices for

their labor and will enjoy a competitive edge. In the absence of laws enshrined by governments to perpetuate discrimination, the market should correct for it over time by penalizing discriminatory employers and rewarding the others. Eventually, the wages of the discriminated will rise.

If jobs have no intrinsic worth, then the comparable worth position has been severely wounded, for it bases its case on precisely such an assumption. What I have argued is that jobs have no intrinsic value within the context of a market economy. Now, that is an important caveat. A competing system, one that sets the prices for all goods, services, and labor by a central planning agency could provide an alternative framework to the market. But would the price of various types of labor be objectively set in such a system? All we could say is that the planners would tell everyone else what each job was worth. Via job evaluations, direct flashes of insight, or whatever methodology they chose, the wages of labor would be set and everyone would abide by those directives. One might call such a system objective in the sense that departures from the assigned wages might be punishable, but using the term in the way we normally do, it seems like rampant subjectivism. . . .

The Value of Work

Another problem with this quest for objective value or worth is that it confuses moral language with economic language. Surely, economists talk about value: they mean by the value of a commodity what it will trade for at any particular time in the marketplace. There is nothing mysterious, no essence that lies buried beneath this market value (at least since the labor theory of value was abandoned).

What the comparable worth people mean by value is something essential to any particular type of labor. They are looking for some higher order moral principle that, irrespective of the market, can compare the work of the plumber to the tree-trimmer to the grocer to the secretary to the nurse. Within our society, there is no agreement about higher order moral principles: about what contributes to the good life; what activities are worthy of pursuit in their own right; what kinds of behavior contribute to the welfare of society. How can we expect individuals in society to agree about how particular jobs contribute to ends, when those ends themselves are in dispute?

Wouldn't it be an unpleasant world if people did agree about values, if those values could be objectively measured as they were exemplified in different jobs, and if they were paid accordingly? Then, if Michael Jackson earned a million dollars for each performance while an emergency room nurse received $20 for her work during the same two hours, we would know that he was really worth 50,000 times as much as she; that is, that society valued her contribution so very much less. We would know, simply by the salary paid to each person in such a society, exactly what his social contribution and, presumably, his social status was. But on a market we cannot even infer that a plumber making $10 an hour is worth more or less to his employer than a teacher who earns the same wage is worth to hers. Such comparisons are vacuous. One's worth, in the moral sense, is not measured in the marketplace by one's wage. Price and salary are economic terms, and they depend upon the available supply and the demand for particular kinds of labor. Value and worth are moral terms, as comparable worth's supporters intend them, and they do not equate well at all with price in the marketplace. Thus, even the market cannot equate the worth (in the moral sense) of one job with another; all it shows is that at any particular time secretaries are paid more or less than zoo keepers.

> *"Any attempt to impose one pattern of distribution as the just pattern requires perpetual interferences with human freedom of action."*

Any attempt to employ "objective" job assessment criteria must be inherently discretionary. That blanket statement stands unrefuted by the comparable worth camp. I believe it is logically impossible for them to surmount this difficulty: for they cannot find objectivity by appealing to the views of experts who, as human beings, bring their prejudices to any assessment; nor can they find it by abandoning the market and embracing central planning, which is nothing more than personal whims enshrined in decrees. Either way, the judgments of bureaucrats or judges would be forcibly substituted for the assessments of those who are the actual purchasers of labor services. This is unavoidable, since there is no intrinsic value to any job. The impersonal forces of the market would have to be replaced by subjective judgments, by the opinions of "experts." Even if these "experts" were bereft of all tastes—which is, of course, inconceivable—they could not implement a system of objective measurement. Where is the metric? None is to be found. While each person can order his own preferences, these separate preference orders cannot be equated. Similarly, different jobs cannot be equated on any objective scale, at least not until everyone is in agreement about ultimate moral values. Even then, their particular application would be open to differences of opinion.

The comparable worth critics are correct: there is no intrinsic value to any job, and, hence, they can neither be measured nor compared.

Most proponents of comparable worth argue that it is not an alternative to the market, that it is like other correctives to the market that have been instituted by government in recent years. I contend that this is false. Comparable worth, unlike the Equal Pay Act, Title VII, and affirmative action, cannot be grafted onto the market. Rather, the market and comparable worth emanate from two entirely different normative assumptions about individual action.

The market exemplifies the assumption that individual consumers ought to be sovereign, that their desires ought to rule the economy. Comparable worth assumes that individuals ought not be the final arbiters of economic life. Some individuals, rather, should place their judgments above those of the rest of their countrymen. These "experts" will ensure that wage decisions are made on equitable, nonprejudicial grounds.

The Equal Pay Act said to employers that you cannot pay women less than you pay men for the same job. Title VII said to employers that you cannot discriminate in hiring, promotion, compensation, and so forth between men and women. And affirmative action said to employers that you must try to advance women, as historic victims of discrimination, to positions in which they had been under-represented. All of these mandates interfered with employers' rights (and employees' rights, too). All limited employers' freedom. Formerly, an employer could hire whomever he liked, pay whatever he liked, and use any criteria for hiring that he wished.

But comparable worth is different. Instead of employers determining their wage scales by evaluating their demand for a certain type of labor and the supply of it on the market, "expert" boards would have to examine the jobs in each firm or government bureau and set wage scales according to the comparability of different jobs. While most comparable worth advocates do not envision one wage board doing this for the entire economy—as the National War Labor Board tried to do during World War II—it is obvious that some national standards would have to evolve or be imposed, either by legislative act, bureaucratic decree, or judicial interpretation. Without such a universal standard, employers would be left in perpetual limbo about how to stay on the right side of the law: they would hang on each turn of the judicial worm. . . .

A Country in Chaos

Furthermore, the institution of a comparable worth scheme nationwide would depend not only on a universal standard and pay boards but, more problematically, on a static view of the economy. Let us suppose comparable worth were put into effect and operated at time t_1 to the satisfaction of its supporters. What would immediately happen at time t_2? A myriad of events would occur to upset the carefully crafted design. Consumer choices, preferences for jobs, availability of resources, and so forth would change. In addition to these causes of change that operate in any economic system, the comparable worth scheme itself would generate market distortions. For example, by raising wages for certain kinds of jobs (that is, those dominated by women), comparable worth would generate a tremendous oversupply of workers for such jobs. But this, presumably, would lead to an undersupply of workers in other jobs. Wages in these understaffed fields would have to rise to attract needed workers. However, such an adjustment would put the female-dominated jobs again at a disadvantage, and their wage rates would have to be increased, again, by the regulators. Thus, more and more economic distortion would be engendered.

"Equality of results . . . seems to be the vision embraced by comparable worth's adherents."

To avoid total chaos, this dynamic view of the consequences of comparable-worth-induced market distortions indicates that the comparable worth wage boards, or the consulting firms operating from firm to firm, would have to be a permanent fixture of our economy. As soon as "pay equity" were achieved, it would be upset in the next instant. Thus, the comparable worth evaluations would be a continuous process, constantly disrupting the economy, causing massive uncertainty, instability, and the impossibility of any rational planning on the part of businesses, workers, or consumers. Many workers, in addition, would be disadvantaged because the continuous reevaluations would limit their ability to gain security through long-term contracts. The only way to avoid these natural consequences would be an attempt to freeze the economy. But, of course, this is impossible: wage and price controls only appear to freeze the economy, while the market simply goes underground. Therefore, I conclude that comparable worth cannot be operationalized. As philosopher Robert Nozick pointed out, any attempt to impose one pattern of distribution as the just pattern requires perpetual interferences with human freedom of action. . . .

Discrimination

Comparable worth proponents believe the market for women's work has been distorted by centuries of discrimination. The market devalues the work of women, and hence it should be supplanted.

The work of June O'Neill and others in demythologizing the wage gap is compelling. It is clear that if women exhibited precisely the same characteristics as men—the same level of education and mix of courses, the same longevity at present employment, the same work force participation levels, and so forth—the "wage gap" would shrink to a "wage pittance" of a few cents, as indeed it has for younger women and single women. The case for massive distortions of the market resulting from discrimination

just has not been convincingly made. A gap of 10%, which can be putatively accounted for by other intangible factors like motivation, goals, and family commitments, simply cannot carry the case for revolutionizing our market system.

Equality of Results

William R. Beer, a sociologist at Brooklyn College, raises an interesting point in trying to assess how important discrimination is in the lives of women (and blacks, too) in the United States. Why not ask the members of the relevant groups how discrimination has affected their lives. Beer cites a study conducted by *The New York Times*, in November 1983, in which they did precisely that. Three questions were posed: "In the place where you work now, do you think you've ever been discriminated against because you're a woman in terms of salary, responsibility, or promotion?" Seventy-seven percent of the women questioned answered "no." "In other places where you have worked, have you ever been discriminated against because you're a woman?" Seventy-three percent said "no." "Has it ever happened to you, that in seeking work, you applied for a job that interested you, only to learn they wanted to hire a man and not a woman?" Eighty-three percent responded "no." Beer concludes that it is false to suppose that a case can be made for systemic discrimination, although individual instances of such discrimination certainly do arise.

But leaving this aside, there is something else fundamentally flawed about the proponents' line of argument. Comparable worth cannot eliminate discrimination from the labor market, and neither can any other scheme, including the market. The purpose of any hiring process is precisely to discriminate. A personnel director does not only look for skills in hiring an applicant. Such intangibles as personality, looks, motivation, and so forth play a factor. Just as any employer discriminates in hiring, so the consulting firms or wage boards would impose their tastes and value judgments. . . .

The labor market as it currently operates in the United States embodies a conception of equality that political theorists call equality of opportunity. All positions in society ought to be open to everyone, without any artificial barriers of race, religion, nationality, sex, and so forth being placed in anyone's way. Where the actual world departs from this model, government intervenes to guarantee the rights of those who have been discriminated against. While equality of opportunity has its problems—it interferes with personal liberty—it is preferable to the view of equality embodied in the comparable worth position. Equality of opportunity is the liberal conception enshrined in the Civil Rights Act and its successors.

Equality of results, or some looser variant of it, seems to be the vision embraced by comparable worth's adherents. As I have argued earlier, the attempt to put such a principle into operation (as

Nozick argued) is doomed to failure. Life will always intervene to upset the carefully balanced apple cart. Even if this were not so, I do not think equality of results is an appealing moral objective. It is contrary to our tradition, going back to John Locke and the natural law theorists, of treating each person as an individual. Equality of results demands that each person be treated as a component of an organic society; the parts must be rearranged and rewarded so the entire organism will be just.

The comparable worth camp might respond that the foregoing is merely an historical argument about Western traditions and is not in itself compelling. I think it is more than that. It is based upon a realization that individuals are different—they have disparate talents, needs, desires, and tastes. These differences cannot be denied. Any attempt to fit such heterogenous beings into one scheme to judge "worth" would involve a massive amount of paternalism: much more extensive and intrusive than the protective labor laws of the late nineteenth century that the comparable worth people so rightly condemn. If individuals freely hiring on the market and individuals freely offering their services determine that dog catchers are "worth" more than nurses and the comparable worth board or court thinks otherwise, then the wishes of countless employers and workers will count for nothing.

"Discrimination is irremediable, and it cannot be eliminated by comparable worth schemes."

Equality of opportunity is more appealing than equality of results because at least it gives more respect to the wishes of individuals and it just tries to guarantee that the process of selection is in some sense "fair." It does not require making independent assessments of the value to society or to a firm of the work of baseball players, laundresses, plumbers, or secretaries. It leaves such decisions to the marketplace.

A Flawed Plan

I have offered several theoretical arguments that question the key assumptions upon which the case for comparable worth depends. These assumptions are either fallacious or they cannot be carried out in the real world without producing chaos. (1) Jobs have no intrinsic worth or value, and, therefore, they cannot be objectively measured or compared. (2) Comparable worth operates on principles that are antithetical to the market. Thus, one must choose either the market or comparable worth. (3) Discrimination is irremediable, and it cannot be eliminated by comparable worth schemes. In fact, comparable worth might exacerbate

the problem of discrimination by replacing the choices of millions of individuals by the view of "experts." (4) Finally, equality of opportunity is preferable on many grounds to the alternative embodied in comparable worth—equality of results.

Ellen Frankel Paul is research director and professor of political science at the Social Philosophy and Policy Center at Bowling Green State University in Ohio. She is also an adjunct scholar of the Cato Institute, a public policy research organization.

"Experts believe that women do best by combining a little of the male game-playing savvy with their natural feminine strengths."

viewpoint **11**

Executive Women Should Stress Their Femininity

Jeanne Toal

Ask most people what it takes to get ahead in a career (besides a little talent and hard work) and they'll tick off unsavory qualities: blind ambition, a false joviality, a this-is-war-take-no-prisoners attitude, a love of besting rivals. Men, through sports, are exposed early to a world that thrives on these characteristics. But not so we women. For most of us, our first job is our first encounter with them. And a lot of us take one look and decide, If that's what it takes to win at the career game, I don't want to be The Big Cheese.

Well, here's some heartening news: There is a good chance that you can act more like yourself—meaning, more like a woman—and still get ahead. In fact, you may be able to make it to the top precisely because of your "feminine" qualities. A growing number of books and seminars now stress that.

So what are these feminine qualities? Compassion, a facility for compromise, a capacity to nurture and an ability to read people well. One widely respected Harvard University study also shows that women are more likely than men to take in a number of details and points of view before making a decision.

More and more experts insist that women suffer when they try to adapt completely to the very different male behavior-style, which stresses winning at everyone else's expense, ignoring colleagues' emotions, not questioning the rules. These same experts believe that women do best by combining a *little* of the male game-playing savvy with their natural feminine strengths.

"In discussion with thousands of successful women—and men—I began to see a new style of power emerging, one that integrates masculine directness with feminine perceptiveness," says Aliyah Stein, M.S., M.F.C.C., a psychotherapist and organizational consultant with a private practice in San Francisco. And, according to Marilyn Loden, management consultant and author of *Feminine Leadership* (Times Books), "The very definition of effective leadership is changing. Skills that women were encouraged to leave behind when they entered the world of management are now being recognized as critical to their companies' long-term health."

The New Style

In fact, some companies now place such value on these skills that they send male managers to seminars to learn them. The National Training Laboratory (NTL) in Arlington, Virginia, for example, conducts over 100 workshops a year to coach executives from Fortune 500 companies and government agencies in sensitivity training. Also, the progressive management styles touted by business gurus like Tom Peters, coauthor of the bestselling *A Passion for Excellence* (Warner), and Robert Waterman, author of *The Renewal Factor* (Bantam), emphasize the importance of such traits. "Quality leadership is about care, people, passion, consistency, eyeball contact and gut reaction," says Peters.

Examples of successful feminine work styles abound in the real world. Sherry Suib Cohen, author of *Tender Power* (Addison-Wesley), cites bosses who benefit from wielding this new power: Cathleen Black, publisher of *USA Today*; Ellen R. Gordon, president of Tootsie Roll Industries; and Lois Wyse, president of Wyse Advertising, are just three.

Of course, not all offices and fields of endeavor are going to be conducive to a more nurturing style. For every Ann Kelsey who succeeds on TV's *L. A. Law* by tempering her hard-nosed ambition with compassionate behavior, there is also an office where only a Grace Van Owen— playing a strictly male game—will excel. But many of us will, at some point, be in situations where we are allowed to be more Kelsey than Van Owen, where we can forget the advice to "get tough," and learn to "think like a man."

Jeanne Toal, "Success and the Soft-Hearted Woman." This article was originally published in MADEMOISELLE, October 1989 and is reprinted with permission.

Following are five scenarios that show how to use a more feminine approach— and why a lot of businesses might be well-off looking for a few good women.

Play *Nice* Politics

For the past two years, Julie has been the assistant marketing manager in a small cosmetics company. Everyone always tells her what a good job she's doing, how deft she is at handling customer complaints and smoothing out organizational problems. So why was she recently passed over for a promotion? Probably, she figures, because her new boss, Anne, hates her. Anne blocks Julie's suggestions—objects to practically every move Julie makes—but won't tell her why, or how she could do it all better. Julie has considered going over Anne's head to complain to the sales manager, but knows that he and Anne are friends.

So Julie takes a different tack. She decides to figure out what's behind Anne's animosity. She realizes that while Anne has an excellent sales record, she knows very little about customer relations—Julie's specialty. Also, there's a good chance Anne is feeling isolated in the office, since everyone in the marketing department took Julie's side when she was passed over for the promotion.

So Julie tries something that—although she doesn't know it—is a perfect example of soft power in action. Instead of waging a war, as a traditional male style might dictate—trying to best or humiliate Anne, or rally others against her—Julie begins to give Anne a sense of inclusion. She tells her in advance everything she plans to do and reviews interactions she has with customers, actually sharing information. In the end, she not only turns an enemy into an ally, but learns a valuable secret: Over lunch one day, Anne tells Julie that her lack of technical savvy is keeping her from being promoted and offers to coach Julie whenever the two have free time. Anne is repaying Julie's favors; by helping Anne, Julie helped herself to get ahead.

"According to some researchers, women may be better able to perceive details and subtle differences in people and then to store these observations for future use."

It used to be thought that the only way to get authority was to take it away from someone else. No longer. A new definition of power includes the powerful act of empowering others. The leader of the future, says Michael Silva, coauthor of *The Future Five Hundred* (NAL), will be one who "converts people and persuades them to shared values." Says consultant Loden, "Feminine leaders understand that controlling others' behavior isn't as productive as encouraging them." And Aliyah Stein further adds, "One of the main skills that women bring to positions of power is the ability to discover another person's emotional agenda. This lets you get what you want by making it possible for another person to get what he wants. This is power without betrayal; this is power that makes you feel good."

Sheila, personnel director for a large medical supply company, is stumped. She's just interviewed two prospective employees for a position in the sales department. One has impeccable credentials, including a recommendation from an assistant vice-president of her firm. The other has less sales experience and no powerful allies in the company, but has swayed her with enthusiasm and marketing ideas.

Should she trust her instinct when the facts warn against doing so? The answer is, yes. She's good at reading people and knows it. But in the business world, it would be folly to decide *solely* on the basis of instinct. What she must do now is search out new information to support it.

Women Better Prepared

So Sheila makes an extra effort to check out the applicant she prefers. And she arranges an informal meeting between her v.p. and her favorite choice. This style reflects a smooth blend of feminine perceptiveness and masculine game-playing.

When it comes to operating on both levels at once, women are better prepared than men. According to some researchers, women may be better able to perceive details and subtle differences in people and then to store these observations for future use—in short, they may be better than men at thinking intuitively. There is growing evidence that innate differences in the structure of male and female brains account for this. Most researchers believe that social conditioning also plays a very important part. Women rely on intuition more than men and can be rewarded for that at work.

Laura's department has grown by leaps and bounds in the past few months, and, to accommodate the growth, she now needs to revamp office procedures. This will disrupt everyone's already tight work schedules. To complicate matters for her, two rivalrous staff members have approached her with separate suggestions for new filing and retrieval systems.

Now, according to the stereotypical male way of dealing with this, Laura would choose one or neither of the two systems, guaranteeing that she would leave at least one person feeling alienated and like he had just finished last in a contest. She might even announce which system was going to be implemented at a department meeting instead of telling each rival in advance and in private.

But she doesn't choose that course. She opts for a far more considerate, conciliatory—and feminine—method. She gathers her entire staff together to discuss more possible reorganization solutions, acknowledging that helpful ideas have already been offered by two employees. The revamping takes time—three weeks rather than one—but the group eventually comes up with a good solution. Because all were allowed to participate, everyone is willing to work a little harder in order to minimize disruption when the new system is put into place. An unexpected bonus is that Laura's department is now a tighter-knit group.

Consensus-building—trying to get people to support decisions while they are being made—is not only an important aspect of feminine nurturing power, but also a recognized, valued management tool. "Some organizational experts are saying that the only way to remedy the production and morale problems dogging American corporations today is to become better consensus-builders," says Loden. "If we're going to succeed, we need to get people involved in shaping the way an organization is going to be operating in the future."

Cathy has a problem: her secretary, Susan. For weeks now, Susan has been coming into work late, making a lot of mistakes. And today Cathy's boss hinted that Cathy is unable to supervise employees adequately. Cathy suspects that Susan has personal problems—perhaps even involving drugs. Should she ask Susan about her life outside the office—or tell her to shape up or get out?

The time-honored male style of power requires that one never get involved in a subordinate's personal problems. A newer, softer approach, on the other hand, would consider a woman's natural warmth and receptiveness a potent asset in this case—and *would* call for delving into what personal factors may lie behind Susan's performance slide.

Cathy tells Susan not only what she suspects but also that she's concerned for her and asks how she might help. After hesitating, Susan confides that her new boyfriend is a heavy drinker, and that the only time they really get along well is when they're drinking and doing cocaine. Cathy kindly insists that Susan get some sort of counseling if she wants to keep her job. Having gathered enough information from Susan, she was able to help both Susan and herself.

Ease Out an Enemy

Janet is an associate editor at a small city magazine. She likes her job. Today, however, she feels vaguely uncomfortable about an upcoming staff meeting, though she can't put her finger on why.

When she walks into the conference room later that morning, her feelings of anxiety increase. This time she pays attention to them. Looking around, she notes that her editor and the publisher are both present, and looking uneasy. She also notices that Eileen, a new writer who reports to Janet, is looking smug.

Something is up, but what? Could it be that Eileen has gone over Janet's head to complain about conflicts the two of them have been having lately? A talented writer, Eileen tended to insist on doing things her way and seemed angry whenever Janet asked her to rewrite something.

"You see, feminine power may be a softer brand of power altogether, but it is still power."

Deciding that she has deduced the problem, Janet starts a discussion about the need for an editor to have control. She then tells everyone about the run-ins she and Eileen have had lately. Both her bosses and the staff leave the meeting impressed with Janet's perceptive and forthright management style. Eileen, however, they now label a complainer, someone not to be trusted. By relying on her gut reaction, Janet was able to cut off a potential backstabber before she gathered much "ammunition," and to defuse a potentially damaging situation.

As much as we may wish otherwise, competition remains an inevitable part of work. Men may take the combative and confrontational behavior they learned on playing fields to office competition, but there is a gentler way to handle a rival. Girls spent just as much time talking with each other about who could and couldn't be trusted, and in the process developed antennae sensitive to subtle facial and conversational cues that help them decide how best to handle people.

You see, feminine power may be a softer brand of power altogether, but it is still power. After all, what else would you call something that gets the job done so well?

Jeanne Toal is a free-lance writer based in Palo Alto, California.

Executive Women Should Develop Masculine Qualities

Patti F. Mancini

I thought I'd begin by drawing an analogy to describe how it feels for a woman to reach a position of power. So, if you're ready for a little mental calisthenics, put on your running shoes, because we're about to compete in an event which I call "The Power Decathlon."

Imagine you're about to run the final race of an Olympic decathlon. As you leave the dressing room and walk down the dimly lit tunnel that leads to the field of the arena, you pinch yourself to prove you're really there.

Who could blame you for seeming skeptical? As a woman, you'd had to buck tremendous odds just to reach a middle management position. But you'd made it, and now, here you were, competing for all the marbles—a female in a field composed almost exclusively of middle-aged white males.

The suspense builds as you step outside onto the track. The festive sights and sounds of one hundred thousand cheering spectators surround you and send your adrenaline skyrocketing.

You reach the starting blocks and scout the scene. As a woman, you'd been relegated to the outside lane: narrow, poorly defined, muddy, and dotted with hurdles and confusing detours. The lanes of your male competitors, on the other hand, are wide, in excellent condition, and free from obstacles. You accept these obstacles as challenges, and vow to press on to victory.

The starter calls the runners to their marks. You take a deep breath, and brace yourself against the block. Your heart pounds in nervous anticipation. The crowd hushes. . . .

Bang! You're off! You hurl down the track, your pulse racing at incredible speeds. The world around you blurs, and the heat of the competition engulfs

you. Perspiration pours down your cheeks . . . into your eyes . . . down your back.

Your shoes slip and slide in the mud, and you struggle to maintain your footing. Your eyes strain in an attempt to define the boundaries of your lane. You leap hurdle after endless hurdle, each one sapping your strength just a bit more.

You've fallen far behind. By the time the race reaches its midpoint, the field is barely in sight. Self-doubt begins to prey upon your mind. Will you give in to it?

Then, just when you're about to give up, you reach down, deep inside, and find your conviction. Suddenly, you're invigorated! You begin to gain on the field. You feel like you're flying; the hurdles and detours seemingly recharging your energy, rather than consuming it.

The race enters its final stretch. You pass one competitor . . . then another . . . then another. As the finish line draws near, you're side by side with the leader. You lunge forward . . . and you've won! The crowd roars. You collapse to your knees, physically drained but emotionally sitting on top of the world.

Those of you who've achieved a position of power can probably attest to that scenario: the inequity of the race women must run . . . the frustrations of the journey . . . but, most of all, that incredible feeling of victory. Once you experience it, you never want to settle for anything less. As the highest ranking female in a company of more than 112,000 employees worldwide, it's a feeling I've had the great honor to experience. And yet, not so many years ago, it would have been thought impossible.

Getting to the Top

Today, however, it's becoming a reality for a growing number of women. We're competing alongside our male counterparts in a wider diversity of career fields than ever before, and the statistics bear testimony to our successes. And while the

Excerpted from Patti F. Mancini, "The Politics of Power," a speech delivered to Women in Management's 1989 Spring Conference, Los Angeles, CA, April 1, 1989.

infamous "Glass Ceiling" continues to block many talented and deserving women from the upper echelons of management, cracks are slowly beginning to emerge.

But that glass ceiling isn't going to shatter itself . . . we're going to have to break it . . . so why should we throw stones? Just what is power, anyway, and why is it so important? What does it take to succeed in a man's world? How do we clear the political hurdles? And, once we've won, how do we stay on top? . . .

A Dynamic Variable

Power is a dynamic variable. It changes constantly during the course of a career. There are those who believe power is never bestowed—that it is, in fact, only taken. This may be true when a person is first attempting to reach a power position. People "take" power through their hard work and good deeds, as well as through influence, strategy, and the right alliances.

But once you've made it into the power structure, the nature of power changes. As former Speaker of the House Tip O'Neill has said, "Power accumulates when people *think* you have power." And that's so true. People's perceptions, regardless of their validity or origins, create their own reality and affect our interactions with others. And a significant factor in people's perceptions of power is a person's title or office. A rose by any other name might smell as sweet, but call that rose a wildflower and just try to get $60 a dozen for them.

My point here is that much of a person's power is inherent in the office they hold, not in the person themself. There's really nothing mystical about it. Work hard, play the game with the boys, and power will come to you.

"Our society raises men to value individual and team sports and competitive situations. Women, on the other hand, are rewarded for being quiet, nice, and even subservient."

But "AH!" as the Bard would say, "There's the rub." The boys don't want to play the game with you. They're not interested in hearing what you have to say. Why? Two reasons. First, it's *their* game, invented by them, for them. Second, they're afraid you'll try to win—that you'll have ideas about ways to improve the game that are different from theirs—and their precious male egos wouldn't like the friction that would cause. So they invent lots of ways to eliminate the competition.

Why, then, do women need power? Because power is freedom. Power allows us to accomplish what is important to us, in the manner that we best see fit. It

separates the doers from the dreamers.

All of us exercise some degree of power in our everyday lives. The good news I bring you today is that everyone can take steps to increase that power and compete in the power decathlon. The bad news is that there are lots of people out there who are either hoping you'll stumble or who plan to trip you up. That's why if you're going to compete with the men in the power decathlon, you'd better be prepared to hit the ground running.

So how do you ensure that you break out of the starting block with the guys and not get left in the dust? By making sure that your power quotient, or PQ, is up to snuff before you ever enter the arena. A power *what*, you ask? I've coined the term, "power quotient," to measure a person's capacity for success. I like to think of it as something akin to an intelligence quotient for success. Its elements are the qualities shared by America's most successful businesswomen.

Lee Gardenswartz and Anita Rowe, in their book, *What It Takes*, identify these qualities as:

—"Four-wheel driven," which I'll call ambition
—"Magnificent obsession," which I'll refer to as enthusiasm
—"Megavision," or vision, for short; and
—"No excuses, just results," which I'll call a results orientation.

Their fifth success factor, "practical magic," is a blend of business savvy, people skills, and the ability to learn from everything. I prefer to include these elements in a more general category called "tools.". . .

You're ready to run in the power decathlon. You brace yourself for the race . . . the gun sounds . . . and still you may trip out of the starting block. Why? Because many women do not possess that one other crucial skill that can often mean the difference between success and failure: a mastery of office politics. It is to this subject that I will now turn.

In the power decathlon, I like to think of office politics as the equivalent of the high hurdles. In this race, you're competing against not just the men, but also the system itself, and even other females.

Office politics is what makes the business world go 'round. It's the day-in/day-out behind-the-scenes maneuvers people engage in in order to influence the course of events in ways favorable to them. It is competition and survival of the smartest. At its root are the structure and rules of military organizations and team sports—"games" that men, but not women, have traditionally played.

The Game and Its Rules

Yes, business is, quite literally, a game. A serious one, but a game nonetheless. And office politics are its rules . . . that's why men are so good at business . . . they understand its rules. And why shouldn't they? They've been groomed for the business world their entire lives. Our society raises men to value individual and team sports and competitive situations. Women, on the other hand, are rewarded for being quiet, nice, and even subservient. Kathryn Stechert, author of *On Your Own Terms: A Woman's Guide to Working with Men*, says it best: "What women often fail to understand is that, vicious as men can be in competitive situations, they are enjoying themselves."

Women who don't think of business as a game, who don't know the rules, or who choose to ignore the politics of the workplace risk jeopardizing their jobs and even their careers. But although the concepts of office politics are foreign to many women, we can learn them as well as men can. It simply requires determination.

I couldn't possibly tell you everything you need to know about office politics. After all, business schools teach entire courses on the subject. What follows, then, is a brief summary of the origins of office politics and a few of the many rules of the political game.

University of Toledo Professors Don Beeman and Thomas Sharkey describe political behavior as one of the most common forms of human interaction. Children learn political behavior by observing, and then imitating, their parents. Parents encourage this process by urging children to understand the political game and its link to survival. During these first, relatively sheltered years of life, children, in particular, boys, learn the concept of competition and its link to rewards.

This link is further enhanced as children enter school, a much more complex and competitive setting, and learn to deal with social groups who control different rewards and have their own set of norms. This process intensifies as children mature and rewards become more and more substantial, until finally the person enters the business world, whose very heart is competition within a highly complex social system.

And it's a cold heart, at that: frequently impersonal, unsympathetic, and intolerant of human frailties. Politics is the way businesses adjust to that fact. And the less results-oriented the field, the more office politics usually come into play.

Learn the Game

The first rule of office politics is that there are no rules. Office politics didn't earn its nasty reputation for nothing, after all. The so-called "rules" of the game often step far outside the boundaries of fair play. Once we recognize this fact, however, there are a number of things we can learn to increase our chances for success.

As I mentioned previously, the basic rules of corporate politics have origins in the military or team sports. Betty Lehan Harragan, in the classic, *Games Mother Never Taught You*, outlines a number of these rules. Examples of military rules include the following:

—Businesses are highly structured, stratified pyramids with a rigid chain of command and a top-down power flow . . .

—Rank is everything, and superiors are entitled to respect. . .

—You have to pay your dues before you can advance up the ranks.

Sports rules cited by Harragan include such items as:

—Rules are our friends

—All players have a position

—Male camaraderie is fun

—Don't talk back to the coach

—You can't win 'em all

—Take defeat in stride

—Nobody's perfect

—Competition itself is the prize, and

—Team glory before personal glory.

"Learn all you can about the structure of your organization—this knowledge can help you determine who has power and is therefore in a position to help you."

These rules shape all aspects of business life, so if women expect to compete, they need to know and understand them. The next rule is that knowledge is power. The key is knowing where to look for information. Don't expect the answers to jump out at you. Robert Jelinek, former executive vice president of Young & Rubicam, Incorporated, describes the typical large business corporation as similar to a totalitarian government. Therefore, in order to gain access to critical information, we need to become, as he termed it, corporate kremlinologists. The corporate kremlinologist relies on three primary means of gathering information: people, paper, and observable signs.

By people, he's referring to the process of networking and plugging into the grapevine—private channels of information we establish that are separate from designated official channels. Obviously, this means building relationships with the people you work with. But it also means establishing working relationships with people in jobs similar to yours in other companies; people in less obvious functions with whom you interact indirectly; people involved in producing products or services related to your own; people in other organizations in your company who can provide different perspectives; and functional executives at the corporate level. . . .

Read Everything You Can

The second means of gathering information is paper. I make it a point to read everything I can get my hands on about my company, its businesses, and its competition. That means reading the technical journals of your particular field, as well as the trade press of your industry. You never know where a great inspiration, or career-saving knowledge, may pop up.

The third means of information gathering is keeping your eyes open for observable signs—that is, information that can be interpreted through careful attention to details. For example, pay attention to who sits next to whom in meetings . . . watch for warning signs of change in the words of key company officials . . . learn as much as you can about the background of key people you deal with so you do not inadvertently offend them . . . and "test the waters," so to speak, before you get into an important negotiation by asking questions and looking for signs that will allow you to gauge what's on people's minds before you begin to deal with them. If "Joe Finance" is having a bad day or seems preoccupied, it's probably not a good time to seek an increase in the department budget.

In short, there are many such signs around you.

Getting Ahead

Once you understand the basics of information gathering, you can apply these techniques to learning some of the other types of rules you need to know, such as organizational rules, unspoken rules, people rules, and gender rules.

Organizational rules are the ways in which organizational bodies are set up. Learn all you can about the structure of your organization—this knowledge can help you determine who has power and is therefore in a position to help you achieve your business and career objectives. Read the company organizational charts. They'll tell you who is supposed to be in power. Pay attention to tell-tale signs such as whose names are regularly copied on important memos. Ask your boss and other co-workers who, outside of your own department, really cares about the work you're doing, and then work to add these people to your network.

Organizational rules also include learning about your corporate culture—the values and image of your company. The company's carefully edited publications, as well as what is written about the company in the media, can help you learn about how your company thinks and how it is perceived by others.

Unspoken rules are more complex and difficult to uncover, but are no less important. One example: is it ever considered expedient to lie? Such rules, as ridiculous as they may seem, are followed as gospel, sometimes only for the irrational reason that "they always have been."

Know Your Colleagues

"People" rules can be especially taxing on your kremlinology skills. To reach the top, you need to be able to get along with all types of people. And your odds will be greatly increased if you take the time to learn about the various personalities of the people you

work with. What makes them tick? . . . What's important to them? . . . What are their hidden agendas—that is, what is each person really after? . . . Who are the favorites of the powers that be—in other words, who always gets their way, and why? . . . Who is considered to be "the enemy" and why? . . . And if these people really are the enemy, why do they act as they do? In short, the more you know about the people you work with, the better prepared you'll be to achieve your objectives and prevent unnecessary detours.

Understand the Male Way

Gender rules are generally established. These are the differences between the ways men and women operate in the working environment. For example, women tend to build trust by revealing themselves. In business, that's not a smart move. Men, on the other hand, use distance as an advantage, and even appreciate the use of intimidation as a technique. Another gender rule is that women tend to get along with each other less favorably than men do at work because they place more value on relationships and are more likely to let loyalty affect their vision. Women have more difficulty in confrontational situations than men. They are more likely to have trouble with delegation and to take on too much responsibility. They are less inclined to take risks, and therefore miss out on valuable opportunities. And they tend to take the game too personally.

"In Megatrends, *John Naisbitt foresees the traditional corporate military hierarchy and pyramid being replaced by networks of people communicating and sharing ideas, information, and resources."*

Harper's Bazaar columnist Nancy Hathaway offers the following advice for neutralizing gender disadvantages:

—Consider all of the potential ramifications of your words before you speak, and speak authoritatively—words like "I guess" and "maybe" make you appear tentative

—Learn about military structure and sports

—Learn to speak, or at least understand, the jargon of the business world, which, according to Betty Lehan Harragan, falls into three general categories: military metaphors, such as "biting the bullet"; sports lingo, such as "ball-park figure," "punting," "scoring," etc.; and, unfortunately, locker room language, which I'll refrain from repeating here

—Learn to hide your anxiety

—Don't act weak or helpless, and especially do not cry

—Mingle with the guys, but do it judiciously; and

—Don't be afraid to use a little humor now and then. . . .

The Future Structure

The good news is that the winds of change are in the air. Experts foresee a shift in the way the game is played: a shift that will actually work in favor of women. In *Megatrends*, John Naisbitt foresees the traditional corporate military hierarchy and pyramid being replaced by networks of people communicating and sharing ideas, information, and resources. He also calls intuition one of the major factors that is beginning to reinvent the modern corporation. Other experts see cooperation, positive relationships, team building, and a win-win approach to negotiations— areas in which females have traditionally been strong —as becoming more commonplace. Just don't expect any miraculous changes to occur overnight. It will take time.

Patti F. Mancini is vice president of public affairs and communications of the Space Transportation Systems Division, Rockwell International Corporation.

"The federal government should be out front in pushing for more child-care options for American families."

viewpoint 13

The Government Should Subsidize Child Care

Patricia Schroeder

Our society cannot decide how to treat the working woman. We have considered child care a "woman's" issue rather than what it really is: a family issue. Our ambivalence stems from two deep-rooted biases: first, we believe that people should not have children unless they can afford them; second, we feel mothers should stay at home with their young children.

Additionally, many people believe that those who "choose" to work don't deserve any assistance in their effort to balance work and family. They see the choice of working outside the home solely as a life-style decision and not as an economic issue. In fact, government statistics tell us that only one woman in 10 will get through life with the option to decide whether she wants to work. The other nine will have to work.

To make progress on child care we must bury these cultural biases. Middle-class women are in the work place because they want the same things for their families that they themselves had as children.

Modern-day economic realities have put pressures on the family that have not been levied on any other generation, and it is quite clear to me that the family unit is breaking down, in large part, because we don't give it any support. We do less than any other industrialized nation: In terms of tax breaks, we would do better raising thoroughbred dogs or horses than children.

Reinforcing the Family

Many people today, as in the past, fight legislation that would acknowledge the kinds of lives women really lead, for fear they will be accused of destroying the mythical family. I think we need to acknowledge the family as an economic unit and basic building block of our society and then get on with reinforcing it.

Today, there are four competing child-care

Patricia Schroeder, "From Star Wars to Child Care," *New Perspectives Quarterly*, Winter 1990. Reprinted with permission.

legislation proposals but they all converge in agreement on one thing: The federal government should be out front in pushing for more child-care options for American families.

• The Bush plan would cost $4-5 billion over the next five years, rising to about $2.5 billion annually after 1993. As far as I'm concerned, this plan does not even come close to providing sufficient options for parents. The gap between family needs and what the Administration is willing to provide is still very wide.

• The Senate plan provides a refundable, supplemental earned-income tax credit to working families with incomes up to $17,000 and a child under four; it authorizes $1.7 billion in fiscal 1990 for grants to states—70 percent to help low-income families pay for child-care services, 30 percent for improving the quality of child care; and it would cost $10 billion over four years, starting in 1991.

• The House Education and Labor Committee plan provides no tax credits; it authorizes $1.78 billion in grants to states for fiscal 1990; it bars money for any sectarian activity, including religious worship and instruction, though it allows the use of church facilities for child care; it bars the use of vouchers, which some states give parents who can then directly pay for child care; and it would cost $14 billion over four years, starting in fiscal 1991.

• The House Ways and Means Committee plan gives families earning up to $21,000 a tax credit of up to $1,217 for one child, $1,504 for two children and $1,790 for three or more children; it provides grants to states by increasing Social Services block grants by $200 million in fiscal 1990, $350 million in 1991, and $400 million in subsequent years; it requires states to use 80 percent of the money to reimburse child-care expenses and 20 percent for administration, training and enforcement of standards; it allows states to set income limits for eligibility; and it will cost $14 billion over four years, beginning in fiscal 1990.

The four proposals mirror the ongoing differences

between liberals and conservatives about the extent of federal participation in child care.

As the child-care proposals show, one of the key differences between conservatives and liberals in the child-care debate lie in their respective approaches to tax credits. Conservatives do not want tax benefits targeted to working parents: They feel that would be an incentive for women to work and would discriminate against women who choose to stay home. Actually, since the first tax code was passed in 1913, our policies have been geared to families in which the mother stays at home. The marriage penalty tax, Social Security discrimination, and limited child-care deductions all penalize working women. If government tax policy had so much influence on the way we live our lives, most women would now be at home.

The truth of the matter is that the economy, not government tax policy, has been the driving force behind the new influx of mothers into the work place. With the huge debt we are running, tax credits for everyone would drain the Treasury, give extra money to those who don't need it, and fail to provide adequate help for those who do. Tax credits should be targeted to those who work.

Married to the Job

For the first time in our history, the majority of American women in their child-bearing years are also working outside the home. In fact, 80 percent of women in the work force are of child-bearing age, and 93 percent of these women are likely to become pregnant during their working careers. The decision to start a family or have another child is no longer simply a private one between husband and wife; it also involves their bosses.

Interest in employer-supported child-care programs continues to rise, but there are obstacles—costs, liability, and the shortage of technical assistance are the three mentioned most often by managers.

"The decision to start a family . . . is no longer simply a private one between husband and wife; it also involves their bosses."

For American companies, the most popular approach to helping parents care for their children has been the establishment of flexible personnel policies: such programs as flex-time, part-time work schedules, flexplace, job sharing, and flexible leave. The programs vary: flex-time allows an employee to choose, within constraints set by the employer, the time when he or she arrives at and departs from work. In job sharing, two people share the responsibilities of one full-time job and prorate the salary and benefits.

For many corporate executives, the term "child care" conjures up an expensive on-site center with high insurance rates and complicated building codes. Yet, most managers don't realize they can offer some child-care benefits that are relatively inexpensive and not burdensome. These include courses to teach parents how to find and evaluate providers; child-care resource and referral services to help parents find good child care; and salary redirection programs, under which specific amounts of money from employee paychecks are withheld, deposited into accounts to pay child-care expenses, and subtracted from the employee's taxable income.

Equality, Not Androgyny

The American women's movement has long been asking for equal rights, but its conception of equality has never had anything to do with "sameness." Pregnancy, after all, is like nothing else.

What we have always maintained is that women bring extra responsibilities to the work place and if women are ever going to have equality, they need equal access to opportunity. If that means instituting special, compensatory policies so that women can compete on an equal footing with men, and still be able to take time out to bear children, so be it.

Take another example: The person who is confined to a wheelchair will never get the job if ramps aren't cut into the curb so that they can gain access to the office building. If they can do the job, we, as a society, need to do whatever it takes to assure that they have the opportunity to succeed.

Redefining "National Security"

Prior to World War II, the mother and father were an economic, as well as a family, unit. It was only after the war that we devised the female ghettoes called suburbs and sent all the men away early in the morning and did not allow them back until after dark. Fathers today are symbolized by the picture on the wall, hung so that the kids remember what he looks like. The way our social structure is currently set up, it will be a very long time before a man dies saying he wished he had spent more time at the office.

I often wonder where our humanity has gone. The US is addicted to technology and often acts like a junkie in its legislative frenzy to buy more of it: We buy B2's; we buy Stealth bombers; but we are not nearly as concerned with the human component of our "national security" strategy.

Our allies, for instance, spend much more per capita for education and health than they do for defense. Japan spends ten times as much for health and education as it does for defense. Not a single NATO [North Atlantic Treaty Organization] country assigns a higher budgetary priority to defense than to the health and education of their citizens. We do.

Between 1975 and 1985, the proportion of Japanese

children living in poverty decreased by half, from 25 percent to 12 percent. During the same period, the poverty rate for American children rose from 19 percent to 24 percent.

Bringing Lives into Balance

If Congress can spend $23 billion on a plane that has never flown, it should certainly be able to do justice to child health and welfare services, parental-leave policies, etc. Indeed, if a child can't bond to its family, it is not going to connect well to its city, its church, or anything else.

The process of bringing our lives, and our legislation, into balance will not force us to nullify or negate; it will force us to reprioritize. People think that we can put the family in the freezer; that children can wait until we have time to be with them. They cannot wait. And though government action is not the prescription for all of America's family ills, to underestimate the role it can play in helping the family accommodate to changed social and economic realities is a dangerous mistake.

Patricia Schroeder has been a member of the U.S. House of Representatives since 1972. She sits on the House Armed Services Committee and the House Select Committee on Children, Youth, and Families.

> *"The obvious and desirable alternative to all these . . . plans . . . is to reduce taxes on families with children and let families spend their own money the way they want to spend it."*

The Government Should Not Subsidize Child Care

Phyllis Schlafly

The obvious intent of the federal baby-sitting bills is so outrageous that even Congressman George Miller (D-CA) admitted that they are really about "creating a lot of state committees to lobby about child care." "A lot," indeed. The bills would create 38,000 local daycare commissions which would empower tax-salaried lobbyists to agitate for more taxpayers' funds.

Congressman Thomas J. Downey (D-NY) described the advocates of federal baby-sitting as people who are "waiting for Lyndon Johnson to come back and sign the bill" and who don't realize that "the era of the Great Society is over." The liberals who want to inflict us with federal baby-sitting are trying to take us back to the Lyndon Johnson era of bigger federal spending for targeted constituencies which, in this case, means the 6 percent of parents who choose secular, center-style daycare (while discriminating against the 94 percent of parents who choose other types of child care such as family care or religious care). . . .

The whole world is moving away from socialism because it is a proven economic and political failure. The demand that Congress move toward government control and regulation of preschool children is coming solely from the liberal media and from the special-interest advocacy groups which are lining up for the gravy train of a new federal spending project.

Tax Relief

Congress should come out of its cocoon and face the real world where Americans want tax relief instead of new spending proposals. The American people didn't want Catastrophic Care for seniors and they don't want Catastrophic Care for preschoolers. The real problem with the liberals in Congress is their lust for Catastrophic Liberalism, and Americans don't want it.

Typical of the many public opinion polls that are

used to make it appear that the American people want the Federal Government to take over baby-sitting was one conducted in 1989 by Lou Harris and paid for by the Philip Morris Companies Inc. It is obvious that the survey questions were written and sequenced to elicit predetermined results.

The Harris/PM survey revealed one of the big problems with this entire issue: the fact that so much advocacy and advice is proffered by people who have no children and therefore have no first-hand knowledge of what it means to bear and care for preschool children. These unqualified, inexperienced promoters of federally financed and federally regulated baby-sitting range from the high-visibility Senator Christopher Dodd (D-CT) and feminist Gloria Steinem to the hundreds of childless staffers on Capitol Hill.

The Harris/PM survey did its pseudo-scientific survey of 2,500 adults and discovered that only 19 percent of respondents had a preschool child. Then Harris surveyed another 1,534 parents of young children, leaving the survey still with a majority of respondents who did not have any preschool children.

The Harris/PM survey used the offensive semantics of "working" versus "non-working" mothers. The notion that fulltime mothers of preschool children don't "work" is the snide attitude of childless feminists who belittle the hard work and real value (to society as well as to the family) of caring for infants and small children.

The 24-page published survey was clearly skewed to promote the idea that the Federal Government should finance and regulate daycare for employed mothers. Buried in the survey, however, was the revealing figure that "53 percent say that children under 6 are cared for at home by their mother." That tallies almost perfectly with Census Bureau figures which report that 54 percent of preschool children are in fact cared for in their own homes by their own mothers.

Phyllis Schlafly, "Look Who's Lobbying for Federal Daycare," *The Phyllis Schlafly Report*, January 1990. Reprinted with permission.

The responsible, caring response to this figure would be to explore ways to increase this percentage, NOT try to provide incentives to reduce this figure by subsidizing federally regulated warehouses for children. When the Harris/PM survey asked what type of care families prefer for preschool children, 75 percent chose care by a child's relative and only 13 percent opted for "daycare groups," a non-precise term that could include neighborhood daycare mothers and religious daycare, both of which would be disallowed under the liberal baby-sitting bills.

Tax Credits Favored

The Harris/PM survey reported that 85 percent of Americans say that the Federal Government should establish daycare regulations. Respondents were not told that all 50 states now have daycare regulations and there is no substantial evidence that they are unsatisfactory.

The overwhelming majority of parents choose family child care in preference to licensed, center-based daycare, anyway, and for good reasons. Family and neighbor child-care providers are usually personally known to the parents and provide environments far less subject to daycare diseases.

If you have the strength to read through to the end of this Harris/PM survey, you find that 97 percent of respondents believe that "parents must play an important part" in selecting child-care alternatives and that 96 percent believe that "parents should be able to choose among several options to decide which child-care program is best suited for their own children." The 3 and 4 percent, respectively, who want to deny parents these rights are probably the child developmentalists who are salivating at the thought of giving control of preschool children to the government.

Despite all the loaded questions, the survey still came out with more people favoring President Bush's child tax credit proposal than not favoring it.

This remarkable result surfaced even though respondents were NOT told that the tax credit proposal is the only federal approach that does not discriminate against mothers who care for their own children or against employed mothers who use daycare by relatives, friends, neighbors, or churches. If respondents had been told the truth about the tax credit plan, it is likely that all respondents would favor it except the liberal bureaucrats and social service professionals who want to increase their own turf and control at the expense of the family.

Content of Bills

The liberal federal baby-sitting bills, which did not pass in 1988 or 1989, are on Congress's agenda for early 1990: S.5 known as the Dodd ABC bill passed by the Senate, and H.R.3 known as the Hawkins-Downey bill in the House. The centerpiece of both bills is the creation of a nationwide system of baby-sitting and

child-rearing by the government in the style of socialist Sweden. They would create a giant daycare bureaucracy, including more than 38,000 separate daycare commissions and a federally controlled daycare system headquartered in the public schools.

Parents who do not want their children raised in government institutions would have to pay higher taxes for this new daycare system. Parents who receive assistance will have little choice over the type of care their children receive. Daycare options would be reduced, since many private and religious daycare centers would be driven out of business by the new daycare network subsidized by the government. This bill is clearly designed to discourage informal child care by mothers, relatives and neighbors.

"Parents who do not want their children raised in government institutions would have to pay higher taxes for this new daycare system."

Here are the major provisions of the Hawkins-Downey bill, as reported by Robert Rector, Policy Analyst of The Heritage Foundation in Issue Bulletin No. 154. Titles I through VI of this liberal baby-sitting bill were written by the House Education and Labor Committee, of which Congressman Augustus Hawkins (D-CA) is chairman.

Title I not only vastly expands Head Start, but more importantly changes its nature from a half-day program for disadvantaged children to a full-day program offering daycare and child development services to the middle class. The family income ceiling for eligibility would be raised from $11,000 to $31,200. The bill authorizes an additional $1.8 billion over four years for Head Start, with up to half going to higher-income children.

Title II authorizes $1.75 billion over four years to create a federally controlled daycare and child development program for three- and four-year-old children inside the public schools. Children from families with incomes up to $33,300 could receive subsidized care under the program, and higher income children could attend if their families pay the costs. Much evidence, such as that developed by David Elkind, author of *The Hurried Child*, warns that such programs can harm rather than help the long-term development of children. In addition, institutionalizing preschool children causes the problem of daycare diseases. The evidence shows that their disease rate is many times higher than for children reared in a home and they are 4.5 times more likely to be hospitalized.

Title III authorizes $2.5 billion over four years in grants to state governments to be distributed to local governments operating daycare programs or to politically selected daycare centers. States must change their daycare regulations to meet the federal standards established by the bill. The bill establishes a national commission to create "model" federal daycare regulations, which would be advisory only for the time being but are obviously intended to be the first step toward comprehensive, mandatory federal regulations.

The bill imposes 183 new daycare regulations on state governments. States can make their regulations more stringent at any time but can never make them more lenient without federal approval, a rule which transfers control over daycare regulation from state governments to the federal bureaucracy.

The bill theoretically permits funds to go to grandmothers and neighbors, but it prohibits states from distributing funds as vouchers. A grandmother would have to enter into a "contract" with the state government to care for her own grandchildren. Thus, few if any grandmothers or neighbors would actually receive any funds.

Title IV authorizes $1.1 billion over four years in grants to state governments to assess daycare needs, establish daycare referral systems, enforce daycare regulations, train daycare workers, and increase salaries of daycare workers in government daycare programs. This title requires each state to create a massive new daycare bureaucracy.

The bill requires each state receiving federal funds to create a "child development council" for each local government, which would add up to 38,000 local child development councils. Each council would be required to submit reports to the state government every four years, thus requiring 120,000 government reports on daycare by the year 2000. These councils would become a permanent nationwide lobbying system for increased federal spending on government regulated daycare.

Regulating Grandparents

Titles V and VI provide $400 million over four years in grants to businesses that operate daycare programs, and grants to state governments to strengthen daycare regulations. . . .

The Social Service Block Grant section of Hawkins-Downey asserts that states are not required to "license" grandmothers, but the bill imposes a vast array of new regulations on grandparents. To receive any daycare funds, a grandmother caring for her own grandchild would have to comply with federally mandated regulations, including building standards in her home, safety standards, nutrition regulations, injury prevention and treatment regulations, child abuse prevention regulations, and health regulations. She would also have to submit to periodic inspection by the government to verify that she is complying with all this red tape.

A neighborhood daycare mother who cares for other people's children would have to submit to all

that, and also be forced to take 15 hours of training every year. She would also be required to provide a written statement of her daycare "program goals" to the parent. . . .

"A grandmother would have to enter into a 'contract' with the state government to care for her own grandchildren."

Titles I, II, and III of Hawkins-Downey explicitly deny funds to daycare providers who include religious activities in their programs. In theory, such religious providers could receive Social Service Block Grant funds, but only if they submit to a wide array of secular state regulations mandated by the bill, including state controls on the selection of program administrators and daycare personnel. Since few if any religious daycare providers would submit to such regulation, Hawkins-Downey effectively denies both Title III and Social Service Block Grant assistance to parents who prefer religious daycare.

Massively Discriminatory

Like the Dodd ABC bill which parents have been opposing for two years, Hawkins-Downey is massively discriminatory against traditional families in which one parent cares for children within the home. Counting all the provisions of the Hawkins-Downey bill, including the grants authorized under Titles I through VI, the SSBG grants, and the nondiscriminatory EITC [earned income tax credit], the Hawkins-Downey bill allocates two and a half times as much taxpayer funding to families that use paid non-parental daycare as it does to traditional families in which the mother cares for her own children. The bill thus contains financial incentives to discourage parental care of children, as well as informal care by relatives and neighbors, despite the fact that this type of care is overwhelmingly preferred by parents and healthier for the children.

Before the Senate passed its daycare bill, S.5, the Senate adopted the Durenberger/Ford amendment, which some Senators have told their constituents would allow taxpayer funding to go to religious daycare. Of course, the religious daycare would have to submit to regulation.

The House-passed Hawkins-Downey bill would prevent taxpayer funds from going to religious daycare unless it becomes wholly secular.

During the floor debate in the House, the House Leadership promised to "fix" the "religion issue" in committee to make it possible for taxpayer funding to go to religious daycare.

But, in order for the religious issue to be "fixed," the daycare bill would have to be amended to require that:

(1) All states must allow parents to get vouchers to buy the child care of their choice.

(2) Vouchers must be usable for religious daycare with religious activities (such as prayer). It is not acceptable to say that vouchers can be used at religious daycare and then require the religious daycare to be secularized.

(3) States must be allowed to exempt religious daycare from state regulations and still receive public funds.

(4) The acceptance of vouchers by religious daycare must not trigger any additional state or federal regulations.

(5) Religious daycare must be eligible for federal grant funds even if the facility displays religious symbols.

Anything less than acceptance of these five points is an attempt to deceive the voters by legislation implying that religious daycare will be eligible for federal money, while at the same time knowing that liberal groups will file lawsuits and get the courts to rule that giving federal funds or vouchers to religious daycare is unconstitutional.

The obvious and desirable alternative to all these complicated, expensive plans to regulate preschool children is to reduce taxes on families with children and let families spend their own money the way they want to spend it.

Phyllis Schlafly is a leading conservative writer on the issues of working women and child care. She publishes The Phyllis Schlafly Report, *a monthly periodical.*

"Family support policy is fast becoming a win-win proposition: good for the working parent, good for the company."

Companies Should Help Care for Children

Sylvia Ann Hewlett

The massive structural shifts of the 1970s and 1980s have made our economy much more dependent on working mothers. In fact, of the 17 million jobs created in the US during the 1980s, two-thirds were filled by women, and the fastest growing segment of the work force is now mothers with pre-school children.

Not surprisingly, issues of family support policy have become central to the lives of modern women. Whether one is talking about private-sector initiatives to provide on-site day care or public initiatives that provide universal access to prenatal care or parental leave, these policies are capable of decreasing the strain in the lives of working women and of enhancing their earning power. In the absence of family support policies, the birth of a child reduces the average woman's future earning capability by 19 percent. Job-protected parental leave and subsidized child care can narrow the wage gap between men and women significantly.

Conflicting Demands

A 1989 *New York Times* poll found that 83 percent of working women were torn by the conflicting demands of their jobs and the desire to do a better job by their children. When asked to name the most important problem faced by women today, the tensions between work and family won the number one slot—issues such as abortion rights were much less important to them.

The reason why this issue is so critical to women is simple: Working mothers continue to bear the main physical burden of running the home and raising the children. In addition, in divorced and never-married situations, women shoulder the lion's share of the financial burden—and it now costs $192,000 to raise a child to 18.

Since women workers have become critically important to the functioning of the economy, it is increasingly in the self-interest of employers to provide benefits and services that ease the burdens of their female employees. Between 1982 and 1988, the number of employers offering systematic child care or parental assistance as part of their benefits package rose from 600 to 3,500.

Even traditional firms have been caught up in the new enthusiasm for family supports. On the face of it, Corning Glass is not an obvious candidate for avant-garde personnel policies. It is a traditional, blue-collar firm that has dominated the small town of Corning, New York for generations. Until recently, its work force was almost exclusively male. However, along with most American corporations, Corning has experienced a steady expansion in the ranks of its women workers. The number of women executives tripled between 1978 and 1988, while the number of women in technical, administrative and manufacturing jobs almost doubled.

This increasing dependence on women workers brought with it one major problem—an attrition rate of female employees that was twice as high as among male workers. This worried top management a good deal—it was bad for image and morale, but it was also bad for business. The Corning managers did some calculations and found that it cost $40,000—including search costs and on-the-job training costs—to replace each worker they lost.

Family Support Policies

Because management suspected that family burdens had a lot to do with the high turnover rate among women, they conducted a survey to find out what kinds of services and benefits would most help their workers deal with the new tensions between work and family life. By the end of 1988, Corning had in place a package of family support policies that included parental leave, part-time work, flexible work

Sylvia Ann Hewlett, "The Feminization of the Work Force," *New Perspectives Quarterly*, Winter 1990. Reprinted with permission.

schedules, job sharing, flexible spending accounts for child care, and a parent resource center that was conducted in collaboration with the public school system.

Until very recently, the list of companies that developed family support policies for their employees was quite short: Merck, American Can, Campbell Soup, AT&T, Polaroid, Control Data, IBM, Johnson & Johnson and Eastman Kodak are famous for their on-site child care, flexible benefit plans and generous parental-leave policies. But as Corning Glass demonstrates, firms need not be progressive or even public spirited to have such policies; all they need do is consult their bottom line. Family support policy is fast becoming a win-win proposition: good for the working parent, good for the company. The needs of the American work place and the needs of American women may be merging for the first time in recent history.

A Win-Win Proposition

Much of the new employment is in the service sector, where high levels of general education, adaptability, and the ability to tolerate a low wage rate are at a premium. Women are more likely to be interested in these jobs and more likely to do well at them. The economy is now operating at low levels of unemployment, and those men who remain out of work often lack the education, attitudes or skills necessary to qualify for the available jobs.

"The needs of the American work place and the needs of American women may be merging for the first time in recent history."

As we look into the future, the pressure is building on corporations to get into the business of family support. The structural facts that conspired to turn family policy into a win-win proposition in the late 1980s are only becoming more urgent as we enter the 1990s. The baby-boom generation is aging and most firms face an extremely tight labor market. According to the Bureau of Labor Statistics, the work force grew at 10 percent between 1980 and 1985, but will only grow five percent between 1990 and 1995. By 1993, there will be 23 million unfilled job slots in our economy. In this labor-scarce world, corporations will find child care and parental leave important weapons in the battle to attract and keep new employees—three-quarters of whom will be women with dependent children.

If the profitability of firms is now tied up with their ability to create a pro-family work place, there is also a collective logic that underscores a new and urgent need for our public policies to do a better job by our

children. America's family problems now threaten the social and economic fabric of the nation. Anyone who has looked at the data recently cannot help but be impressed by the severity of the situation:

- 21 percent of all children are growing up in poverty.
- 28 percent of our teenagers leave high school without graduating, marginally literate and virtually unemployable.
- 49 percent of divorced men neither see nor support their children in the wake of divorce.

Oddly enough, one of the best statements of what we should do about these massive problems has come out of the business community. In 1987, the Committee for Economic Development (CED), a group of 200 CEOs [chief executive officers] and business executives, published a study entitled *Children in Need*. The primary focus of this study was that 30 percent of American children are facing major risk of educational failure and lifelong dependency. The arguments put forward by the CED are compelling:

Poverty-ridden, neglected children grow into problem-ridden youngsters who are extremely difficult to educate and absorb successfully into the work force. Not only does this increase welfare and prison costs, it also seriously undermines the economic strength of our nation. The US is moving into an era of intense competition. In the 1990s, maintaining our domestic and international markets in the face of fierce rivalry from low-cost producers is going to become even more difficult. The prospects for keeping our competitive edge are slim, unless we increase both our rate of productivity growth and the quality of the products we make. Both these goals are critically dependent on the caliber of our future work force and on our ability to educate and train young people. Schools should do more, but they will continue to fall short of the mark unless we strengthen families. Schools alone cannot compensate for the tasks that burdened parents no longer perform.

Costs and Benefits

The CED study calls for a major new commitment to child-welfare and family supports by the government and the private sector. The report is particularly eloquent in presenting the cost-benefit arguments for early intervention in the lives of families. Improving the prospects for mothers and children through prenatal care and early childhood education, for example, is not an expense but an excellent investment—one that can be postponed only at a much greater cost to society.

This year's high school dropouts will cost the nation more than $240 billion in lost earnings and foregone taxes over their lifetime, and this does not include the billions more for crime control and welfare expenses. To use the language of the report: "The nation cannot continue to compete and prosper in the global arena when more than one-fifth of our children live in poverty and a third grow up in ignorance. And if the nation cannot compete, it cannot lead."

In the 1970s, feminism concentrated on pressuring men to share in responsibilities on the home front—with very limited success. Indeed, not only do married men do rather little housework, but divorced and never-married fathers routinely abandon their children.

Economic Facts of Life

Feminism in the 1990s should focus some prime energy on sharing the costs and responsibilities of child rearing with the private sector and with government. For the first time, the hard-edged logic of the bottom line is on our side.

The economic facts of life in the 1990s will conspire to make mothers and children scarce and valuable resources, assets that businessmen will be loathe to neglect or squander. Woman power will have to be utilized more efficiently if we intend to cope with the looming labor shortages of the 1990s, and children will have to be cared for better if we are going to survive as a competitive economy.

Sylvia Ann Hewlett is a professor of economics at Sarah Lawrence College in Bronxville, New York. She is the author of A Lesser Life *and* The Costs of Neglecting Our Children.

Public Schools Should Help Care for Children

Anne Mitchell

The misperception that early childhood education and child care can be discrete services is fast becoming a thing of the past. Programs for young children cannot be one or the other; any early childhood program provides both education and care. These two functions are inextricably bound together; children cannot be well cared for without learning, and they cannot be educated well without being properly cared for.

Probably the most prevalent form of early childhood education experienced by children today is called child care. Parents judge programs for their young children in terms of both their present and their future value—how much their children enjoy the program right now and whether it will help them get off to a good start in their school careers. Parents don't generally separate their demands for care and education. They want both in the same program, in a convenient location, and at a price they can afford. As parents well know and policy makers are beginning to understand, the old distinctions between child care and early education have become so blurred as to be meaningless. . . .

Focus on Young Children

In the 1980s, children under age 5 have clearly made it into the national spotlight. The National Governors' Association Task Force on Children believes that current investment in the health and education of children is linked to the nation's future international competitiveness and calls for a comprehensive approach to child development, beginning with prenatal care and followed by preschool education coordinated with affordable child care. Many governors have put programs serving the needs of children high on the agenda in their state-of-the-state messages—from the Children's Agenda in

Oregon to the Decade of the Child in New York. The National Conference of State Legislatures reports that legislators on human services committees rank child care and early childhood education as top issues for 1990. . . .

The current high level of interest in early childhood programs stems from at least five different sources: 1) the increased demand for child care from the growing numbers of working mothers in all income groups; 2) concern about present and future productivity, international competitiveness, and the changing nature of the work force, which will include more women and be characterized by greater ethnic and racial diversity, as the minority becomes majority; 3) the centrality of child care to efforts to move mothers off AFDC [Aid to Families with Dependent Children] support and into the labor force; 4) a desire to provide a better start for poor children in school and in life; and 5) an accumulating body of evidence that high-quality early childhood programs have long-term positive effects for disadvantaged children and high cost/benefit ratios (on the order of 5 to 1). These varied motivations for interest in programs for young children are strong and intertwined with one another. Alone and in combination, they have already resulted in new policies and programs and will lead to still more.

But where is the system within which to implement these policies? Where can these programs be institutionalized? Unlike other current educational concerns—such as improving math literacy or increasing high school graduation rates, for both of which the clear focal point of public concern and policy action is the public school system—there is no readily apparent early childhood system in which to implement and institutionalize new policies and practices. However, there is a system of sorts, although it is not an intentionally planned one.

Programmatic responses to various interests—child care for all families (or just for welfare recipients),

Anne Mitchell, "Old Baggage, New Visions: Shaping Policy for Early Childhood Programs," *Phi Delta Kappan,* May 1989. Reprinted with permission.

education for poor children, the future of the work force—now emerge from the efforts of many individual early childhood organizations, acting under various auspices (public, private, for-profit, nonprofit, secular, and religious) and funded from public sources at all levels of government and from private sources (mainly parents). In the U.S. today, there are nearly 350,000 early childhood organizations, including the estimated 197,000 private homes offering day-care services.

Examined from an ecological perspective, the current array of providers of early childhood services forms an ecosystem of sorts, sometimes called the early childhood community. The term *ecosystem* implies that the many subsystems of the community are interdependent. If one part changes itself (or is changed by outside forces), the other parts of the ecosystem necessarily change in response.

The early childhood ecosystem has evolved over time and consists of all child-care and early-education services, whether public or private, religious or secular, half-day or full-day: whether called play school, nursery school, or prekindergarten; whether housed in a public school, in a storefront, or in a private home. What the program is called and where it is housed are not indications of its quality. Rather, name and location merely indicate the present purpose or intent of a program (i.e., "nursery school" generally implies part-day, while "day-care center" usually means longer hours) or give clues about its historical origins (e.g., "day nursery" implies origins in the day nursery movement of the early part of the century, while Head Start obviously indicates a more recent program, probably dating from the mid-1960s). Regardless of nomenclature, all these programs serve young children, they are more alike than different, and each has the potential to offer good early childhood services.

Too Few Services

However, the components of the existing early childhood system—the child-care centers, the private day-care homes, the nursery schools, and other formal and informal services—are simply too few and too poorly supported to educate and care for all young children. The supply of services must be expanded throughout the ecosystem. Some national education groups, notably the Council of Chief State School Officers and the National Association of State Boards of Education (NASBE), have recognized the need for equity among the many parts of the early childhood system. The report of the NASBE Task Force on Early Childhood Education notes:

> We have a diverse, underfunded, and uncoordinated system for delivering programs to young children. Public education leaders can be a powerful and constructive force for strengthening this system. If they act in partnership with other early childhood programs, our chances for increasing and maximizing resources and quality

in *all* settings that serve young children will be greatly improved. (Emphasis added)

Public schools have been a part of the early childhood system for years—albeit a small part. Since 1984, however, their role as providers of programs for prekindergartners has grown and will probably continue to expand. A useful way to look at the situation is this: the early childhood system is not moving into the public schools; rather, the public school system is a part of the early childhood ecosystem whose role is expanding.

"The components of the existing early childhood system . . . are simply too few and too poorly supported."

Public schools will continue to provide services to young children through the current federal categorical programs, such as special education and Chapter 1 with its new Even Start program. Public schools will continue to offer child-care services funded through state-subsidized child-care programs, as some now do in many states. Public schools will continue to provide a portion of Head Start programs; currently, about one-fifth of all Head Start programs are operated by the public schools. An increasing number of public schools, mainly in large urban school districts, now offer child-care services to students who are parents, and the number will probably increase as a result of provisions of the Family Support Act of 1988 that deal with education for young parents. This population—student/parents and their very young children—can be logically and easily served by the public schools. In fact, the majority of existing programs for these young parents are housed in public schools.

The current array of state-funded prekindergarten programs will continue to expand slowly, as annual appropriations increase and as a few more states create new programs. Some states will expand their programs more rapidly than others. . . .

It seems likely that most prekindergarten programs will continue to focus mainly on poor or at-risk children. Most will be operated by public schools. However, 13 states currently permit agencies other than public schools to operate state-funded prekindergarten programs, and there is a clear trend toward broader definitions of eligible providers.

A Modest Shift

There will probably be a modest shift away from part-day and toward full-day programs, as the need for longer hours (to meet child-care demands) is recognized. Programs in only five states (Massachusetts, Vermont, Illinois, both of Florida's programs, and New Jersey's two newer ones) now clearly permit the funding of prekindergarten programs that last for the full working day. Some states will emphasize longer hours to cover the full working day in the expansion of their prekindergarten programs, as Gov. Mario Cuomo of New York has proposed.

State policy makers are just beginning to perceive child-care programs as educational opportunities for young children and to recognize the child-care function that so-called educational programs fulfill. Based in part on this new awareness, some states will move toward coordinated approaches that unify early education and child care, such as the Child Development Coordinating Council established in Iowa for fiscal year 1989, the Office of Early Childhood Services being discussed among legislators in New York, and Virginia's Council on Child Day Care and Early Childhood Programs, described as "a major new approach linking together the child-care needs of the labor force and the developmental needs of children at risk."

Guiding Principles

The essential question facing policy makers is, How can we improve the quality of and increase access to early childhood programs for all children—but especially those who are disadvantaged? Any answers we come up with must take account of the needs of children and their families and at the same time understand the early childhood system and recognize its ecological nature.

Children: quality, continuity, and comprehensiveness. From the child's perspective the elements necessary to create good policy are the overall quality of the program and the continuity and comprehensiveness of the services. Quality in an early childhood program consists of five essential elements:

● small group size—for 4-year-olds, for example, between 15 and 20 children;

● favorable staff/child ratios—for 4-year-olds, at least one adult for every eight to 10 children;

● well-trained staff—a thorough understanding of theories of child development and of principles of early childhood education, coupled with direct experience working with young children;

● curriculum—a clearly communicated philosophy of education that is based on theories of child development and that is supported by training and good supervision; and

● strong parent participation—frequent communication between parents and teachers, a variety of ways for parents to participate directly in the education of their children, direct parental influence on the governance of the program, and attention to the needs of parents.

Beyond the obvious fiscal resources necessary to implement a good early childhood program, vision and commitment on the part of its leader are required. The quality of leadership—whether from the director of a single center, the principal of an early childhood school, or the coordinator of a school district's early childhood programs—is directly related to the overall quality of the program for young participants.

"Continuity and comprehensiveness are also essential aspects of high-quality programs for young children."

Continuity and comprehensiveness are also essential aspects of high-quality programs for young children. Continuity has two dimensions: 1) the number and ease of transitions made by children in a given day and during a given year and 2) the compatibility of philosophies and curricula among the different programs that a child takes part in over time. If a child is in a stable group of children, with the same staff members for most of the day in the same location, and with a stable teaching staff throughout the program year, that program has a high degree of continuity. If a child experiences changes from year to year that are smooth and understandable, continuity is also high. However, if changes are abrupt and disturbing during a day, over the course of a year, or between successive years, continuity is low.

A comprehensive early childhood program is one that provides other necessary services in addition to those that are strictly intellectual or academic. At a minimum, such comprehensive services include:

● health services, such as screening for developmental delays and physical examinations (or other direct health services) provided by a doctor, nurse, or dentist;

● social services, usually provided by a social worker, such as referral to community or governmental agencies that can provide needed assistance; and

● nutrition services, which means the provision of meals and snacks during the program's hours that satisfy the major portion of children's daily nutritional requirements.

Finally, transportation can be a critical support service. A child who can't get to any program at all won't derive any benefit even from a good program with comprehensive services.

Parents: quality, participation, affordability, and accessibility. Because parents want the best for their children, good policy from the perspective of parents rests on the overall quality of the program for children. Parents want programs that are good for their children and that respond to their own needs—the need to work or to continue their own education, the need to be good parents, and the need to be involved in their child's education. For most parents, these needs and desires translate into demand for programs that cover enough hours each day, that provide year-round services, and that give parents opportunities to be involved while balancing work and family responsibilities.

Parents also want choices. Not all families need or want the same services for themselves and their children. Parents deserve choices that reflect the cultural diversity of our nation, the full spectrum of family values regarding child rearing, and the differing needs of individual families. In addition, parents want affordable, conveniently located programs that are easy to find, easy to choose, and easy to use. Many parents prefer having all their children in the same location.

From the parents' perspective, early childhood policy is about ways and means: ways to identify good programs, ways to locate the ones that reflect their family values and needs, and ways to choose the best ones for their children—and the means to pay for the good programs of their choice.

Early Childhood System

Early childhood ecosystem: quality and unity. From the perspective of the early childhood system, public policy must be guided by principles of quality and unity. Delivering good programs to children is the objective. Many members of the early childhood system have demonstrated their ability to provide high-quality early childhood services; others have clear potential to do so, with some help.

There is growing concern about the quality of all programs for young children—both in public schools and in other settings—and a number of questions are being asked frequently. Is the program appropriate to the developmental stages of the children in it? Are staff members well-trained? Are there enough of them? Do they remain on staff long enough to produce a stable program for children? A number of questions about the content of early childhood programs have also been raised, specifically with regard to programs in the public schools. Should the curriculum be academic or cognitive or developmental? Should it be some combination of these? Should it focus on school readiness or on child development?

No single kind of early childhood program has a monopoly on quality. Community-based, nonprofit programs are not inherently better than community-based, for-profit programs. Nor are programs operated by the public schools necessarily better or worse than those operated by other agencies. There is much more variation in quality from state to state or from one version of a program to another than among different programs.

The problem of quality is a systemwide issue. Legislative solutions must recognize this fact and deal with improving the quality of early childhood programs throughout the system. It may be necessary to target a larger-than-proportional share of resources to some individual programs in order to produce reasonably good programs throughout the system. The goal is to insure uniformly high quality for every child—no matter where or by whom or with which funds an early childhood program is provided.

"The goal is to insure uniformly high quality for every child."

The early childhood system is an ecosystem. Changes in one part of it affect the other parts—particularly on the community level. For example, when a public school district rapidly expands a program for 4-year-olds, qualified teachers are drawn out of other kinds of early childhood programs because the salaries in the public schools are higher. This only exacerbates any existing staffing shortages in the community. For the system to remain in balance, new policies must take into account the entire system and must be implemented slowly and carefully. Broadly conceived coordinating mechanisms that simultaneously operate on and connect with federal, state, and local levels of government must combine with maximum local flexibility in planning and implementing early childhood programs. In short, an optimal early childhood policy would respond in the best interests of the child, of the family, and of the ecosystem. . . .

The ideal federal bill would take the family's perspective. Parents want affordable programs that are compatible with their values and that combine care and education in one convenient location. All families deserve choices among sound alternatives—and enough money to exercise their right to choose what's best for their children.

There is a clear need for federal action, as this nation begins to shape an agenda for early childhood programs. Federal leadership can provide a model for integrating the care and education of young children that states can emulate as they continue to develop their own early childhood policies. Policy makers at all levels will need to craft solutions that take account of the perspectives of the child, of the family, and of the early childhood ecosystem. Community institutions of all sorts will have to shoulder their share of the responsibility for making high-quality early childhood programs widely available and readily accessible. And public schools must be partners in that effort.

Anne Mitchell is associate dean of the Division of Research, Demonstration, and Policy at Bank Street College of Education in New York City, and codirector of the Public School Early Childhood Study. She is also a coauthor of the book Early Childhood Programs and the Public Schools: Between Promise and Practice.

"Children have [a] . . . basic right to have a full-time mother!"

Mothers Should Care for Children at Home

Gerald F. Kreyche

Baby M no longer is in the news. Many states have legislated against surrogate mothers and, for the most part, the traffic in human biology has stopped. However, is there a new and more subtle surrogacy issue taking its place—namely, universal day care for children? While this is not a biological surrogacy, it is a kind of new social and psychological surrogacy. Is such surrogacy an idea whose time has come or one that ought to be nipped in the bud for the sake of child, family, and country?

Certainly, the care and upbringing that children received from their own parents in earlier times has diminished considerably today and, with it, the bonding between parents and children. The notion somehow has taken root that not only the education of the young, but their parenting as well, ought to be the function of the school system, for most, a public agency. The teaching of manners, the assurance of a nutritious meal, and instruction about not only biological sex, but safe sex, are a few examples of new responsibilities foisted upon an already overloaded educational system. Gradually, the same trend toward parenting—being someone else's job other than the parents'—has worked its way into pre-kindergarten, pre-school, and day care for those six weeks old and up.

Operation Head Start was established years ago to help the disadvantaged achieve near-equal status when they began regular admission to school. However, the much ballyhooed program fell into disfavor and studies questioned the results claimed for it. Nonetheless, poor families recognized it as an important baby-sitting facility and political pressure was exerted to continue and increase its funding.

The issue of day care, often identified with glorified baby-sitting, is in the fore today. One reason is that women are marrying later in life, often after first

establishing themselves in a career or decent paying job. When these women have a baby, they understandably are loath to give up their position and the extra income to get their own head start on a home, second or third car, and other good things in life. They still strongly desire the more luxurious accouterments of married life without children, such as frequent vacations, nights out for fancy restaurant fare, plays, etc. In short, they want it all and believe they can have it. I am, of course, describing the yuppies who now find the "in thing" is to have a child.

Woman as Nurturer

With such an example before them, other women, most of them mothers, also have decided to enter the workforce to get their share. *The American Demographic Magazine* reports that half of all working women who are new mothers and two-thirds of working women over 30 who have a new baby are back at work before their offspring are a year old. Further, two-thirds of women with pre-school children are working mothers. The trend continues. The Bureau of Labor Statistics estimates that, by the year 2000, women will account for some 14,000,000 of the expected 21,000,000 new workers. Whether married or not, women presently are or shortly will become a major part of the U.S. workforce. Aware of this and anxious to score political points, legislators have presented over 100 bills to Congress that deal with working mothers and child care.

Feminists may not like the phrase "their children," but whether correct or not, civilization and our culture still view the woman as the chief nurturer of children in a family. (This is almost universally the case in the ghettos, where some single parents have produced offspring from a wide variety of men.) The courts also have indicated this in decisions as to who wins custody of the children in divorce cases. Informally, we seem to acknowledge the mother's greater importance in this role by a much deeper observance of Mother's Day than Father's Day.

This does not mean that the role of fathers isn't important. Fathers are not the issue. Instead, the argument is that, if the function and obligation of doctors is to doctor and educators to educate, the function and obligation of mothers is to mother.

"There's no substitute for children being parented at home."

If we would believe what the media reports, often quoting from women's pressure groups or politicians running for office, the issue of universal day care already is a closed one and it is only a matter of how best to implement the idea that would be an anathema to oppose. In some ways, it seems true that the *idea* (but not yet the reality) of day care for children as a nationwide phenomenon is here and will continue to grow. Presently, there are 10,500,000 children under six being cared for by people other than their parents, and this number is increasing. The few who oppose rapidly expanding day care already are labeled by the new McCarthyites of feminism as slavish followers of Phyllis Schlafly, who views day care as a "warehousing of children." The men and fathers who oppose it are dismissed summarily once again as demonstrating a knee-jerk reaction as chauvinist pigs.

The feminists argue that all women, whether mothers or not, have a God-given right to a full-time job, and taking care of their own children interferes with this fundamental right. In no way do they address the poignant plea that children have an even more basic right to have a full-time mother! (Interestingly enough, *Good Housekeeping* has had the courage—temerity, women liberationists would say—to run a full-page ad in the business pages of leading newspapers showing a mother with two young children lovingly clinging to her skirt. The ad labeled her the new revolutionary—a traditionalist upholding the values of husband, children, and home.)

Benefits of Day Care

We even are asked by the promoters of universal day care to consider the many benefits it will confer upon society. High officials in government give support to the case, thereby gathering women voters to their party. Their concern, they say, is to recognize the rights of women. Instead, do they secretly and avariciously yearn for the additional tax dollars the government will receive with the increased number of women available for work?

Corporate day care centers, in some cases, already have beaten the government to the draw. The Heller Construction Company of New Jersey has opened the John Kenny Day Care Center in its industrial park, spending $800,000 and subsidizing it with $16,000 a month. Their workers sing its praises. The Gertrude B. Nielsen Center, Northbrook, Ill., recently opened, at a cost of $4,000,000, a not-for-profit center open to all village members. Throughout the country, many hospitals now offer such day care for their employees' children, and the employees pay for this service with pre-tax dollars.

What is the benefit to industry? It is nothing less than self-enlightened interest—namely, to curb the absenteeism and avoid a loss of productivity and profit. One working mother in Denver praised her company for making a day care center available and enabling her to nurse her child at lunchtime. Another declared how nice it was to take her three-year-old to work with her. Yet, somehow, it seems like these women are visiting their institutionalized children—a strange phenomenon indeed.

Private day care centers are everywhere. When we look at the infants, we see them sucking pacifiers, holding on to their "blankies," sleeping on their mats, slopping paint on paper, or sitting in circles and playing games like "Simon Says." Perhaps the motive of such centers is altruistic, but most would agree that a handsome profit accrues to those who become social surrogate mothers. Prices vary greatly, but average costs are $200-300 per week and may exceed $500. Subsidized corporate centers often charge as little as $50 per week, but the estimated cost of quality Federal centers would come to $6,000 per annum.

Child, Family, Nation

There can be no question that some day care must be provided for those unable to rear their children, because the parent(s) must work to make ends meet. However, the near-universal extension of such a program demands some hard examination. In virtually all of the arguments for universal day care, the most important issues never are brought up: "Is it good for the children?"; or "Is it good for the family?"; or, lastly, in a time of national family breakdowns, "Is it good for the country?" So seldom are these questions asked that they sound shocking at first.

Is it good for the child? Proponents insist that day care makes the child more independent, that parent and child are happier to see each other at the end of the day, and the children are introduced sooner to the outside social world—a world where they eventually have to reside anyway. Also, the children learn songs, games, art, and other important things that the mother might never teach them.

Yet, more often than not, this is a rationalization of a conscious choice of giving priority to work over child-rearing. There is much legitimate guilt around to substantiate the charge. Although it is only anecdotal, the beneficial claims are countered by a couple who ran a pre-school and day care center. After three years, consulting their conscience, Wendy and

William Dreskin closed their center, declaring, "There's no substitute for children being parented at home."

There is a downside to day care that only occasionally sees the daylight of publicity. The facts are indisputable, not only to investigators, but also to common sense. Psychiatrists speak of the day care child as experiencing an "alienation-separation syndrome," and one doesn't have to have a Ph.D. to know what that means. It is the direct cause of a lack of self-worth and self-control, as well as emotional and behavioral problems that are masked under a thousand guises. Writing in a *Chicago Tribune* guest editorial, Edward Levine, a social psychologist, summed it up by asking rhetorically, "Can young children develop a loving, trusting identification with part-time parents who give so little love and affection?" His answer was an unequivocal no!

Moreover, it doesn't take a medical doctor to know that it is not healthy for the very young to be subject to the respiratory ills or various contagions to be found in the world outside the home. Kindergarten is soon enough for their immunity system to be tested and built up.

Parental Guilt

Is day care good for the family? Even columnist Ann Landers, who usually seems to side with women on most issues, says that day care means a great deal of worry and guilt for working parents. Amen!, one might say. If it didn't, we really would be in trouble. A child in day care is a child at risk, not that minimum risk isn't present in the home also.

Working parents, to make up for a lack of attention, tend to lavish gifts on the child as a salve for their own stricken consciences, that just won't be silenced. The conscience knows the falsity of such subterfuges as "quality time" and keeping "in touch" by telephone with latchkey children. Loving gifts are no substitute for mother's loving arms. The very young in day care commonly exhibit a clinging syndrome when with their parents, innately afraid of the next separation. This is hardly the development of independence. Findings presented at a recent International Conference on Infant Studies showed that among the bad things coming out of full-time day care were poorer study skills, lower grades, and diminished self-esteem, and that is bad for the family.

Is universal day care good for the country? We only have to look around us, regardless of wealth or class, to see that the stability of marriage, home, and family severely is threatened and that its underpinnings are being eroded and washed away by changing mores and morals. The causes are legion: drug and alcohol abuse, unfaithfulness to marriage vows, the general age of non-commitment and of looking out for "number one," as well as the siren call to hedonism, which proclaims on bumper stickers, "If it feels good, how can it be bad?"

T. Berry Brazelton, a Harvard professor of pediatrics, the Dr. Spock of the 1980's, warns: "Our culture is in grave danger because we're not paying enough attention to strengthening the family." In an effort to begin doing so, he has lent his assistance to a new parent lobby group known as "Parent Action." Unfortunately, he looks toward big government as the way to solve the problem. Meanwhile, in an aside to working mothers, he tells them to "cheat a little on the job" so they will have more energy for their children when home. I am sure all employers would look askance at that!

Likely Consequences

What are some likely consequences of a universal day care program, besides making it easier for parents to shirk their personal responsibilities? One is that somebody will have to pay for such a program. This would be no volunteer kibbutz, which itself is failing badly in Israel. Non-parents are sure to ask why they should be taxed to subsidize the two-career family who wishes to have children. The question is a fair one. Few would object to subsidizing the poverty-stricken, the homeless, or those down on their luck. This is a matter of justice for those who momentarily are unable to help themselves. However, to subsidize day care for the two-career family is something else again.

Another sure consequence would be the additional call for "night care," as we soon could expect to hear charges of discrimination against night workers who number in the hundreds of thousands and who would want their share of the Federal largess.

"Non-parents are sure to ask why they should be taxed to subsidize the two-career family who wishes to have children."

Today, there are 700,000 unmarried couples with children, and we know how they would take to day or night care to ease their already, but freely chosen, burdensome existence. What about teenagers who become pregnant? The burden of child care, if not actual child-rearing, surely will be moved to the government. Instead of the present situation where the teenager's mother or grandmother cares for the child, all the young mother would have to do is to flash her "green card," the magic wand of the welfare world.

The armed services, which see more and more married men in their enlistment, counsel all married couples about budget matters in their home life. Practically the first thing taught is how to make a list of needs and wants and how to distinguish between the two. The issue of universal day care would not be here today if mothers learned and followed such a distinction. Does one really need a second or better car if only one of the spouses works? Does one need to eat out at restaurants several times a week? Does one need those several quickie vacations every year?

Choices and Responsibilities

The bottom line is that, when one makes a decision, one should take the consequences and obligations that follow. If one chooses the possibility of motherhood, under the right conditions and in itself a wonderful choice, one must accept the full responsibilities. That means personally to love, nurture, and provide for that child and not to shove those responsibilities onto others because working outside the home is less tedious and less boring than changing diapers and feeding little mouths that, often in playful spirit, spit back their food. Even the animal kingdom obeys this fundamental law of taking care of its own. It is for the good of the individual and the good of the species.

Yes, motherhood is a burden. Its sorrows and work often overshadow its joys. Certainly, it is a sacrifice and totally demanding. No one can deny this. Also, no one can object to the need for getting some time off from full-time mothering, whether by getting baby-sitters or having an older child spend a day or so a week in some kind of nursery school or day care center. However, calling a spade a spade, regular and full-time day care, other than that required by extenuating circumstances, favors work rather than one's offspring, and that is a terrible thing for children, family, and country.

Gerald F. Kreyche is a professor of philosophy at DePaul University in Chicago, Illinois, and the American Thought Editor of USA Today, *a monthly magazine published by the Society for the Advancement of Education.*

"Women-church desires to bring about genuinely inclusive communities of women and men in the ecclesia of Jesus Christ."

Feminist Theology Strengthens Christianity

Miriam Therese Winter

In November 1983, approximately 1,400 women, most of them Roman Catholic, met in Chicago for a conference called "Woman Church Speaks." That gathering of women who together envisioned and to some extent modeled a church liberated from patriarchal bondage marked a turning point in the women's movement in the United States. For the first time, women whose common heritage was one of disappointment and dissent collectively claimed to be church. They shared with one another their experience of spirituality, sexuality and survival in the church and in society, and went forth as an exodus community coming out of exile within and in some instances beyond the institutional church. In October 1987, over 3,000 women joined the "Women-Church Convergence" in Cincinnati, under the theme, "Claiming Our Power." In the four years between conventions, many had found meaning in the wilderness as they wandered with companies of women of faith and sipped from nourishing springs. Some had grown skeptical of finding a promised land. Most seemed grateful for whatever manna they had found to meet their needs.

It is difficult to assess the impact of the women-church movement—which appears to comprise only a small number of women—on the larger church. While many more claim membership in women-church than convention statistics might imply, women-church is a modest initiative. It is a national network of feminist base communities and a coalition of feminist organizations that seek to support one another in living out of their own faith experience. Any women's group with three or more members can, if it so desires, call itself women-church. Some (not all) of these groups choose to be listed as part of the national network. The women-church movement is not concerned with membership, growth, structure or

institutionalized permanence, nor is it a separatist movement. Those who have found hope through association with women-church know it as an initiative of the Holy Spirit among those who are religiously marginalized and oppressed; it provides respite in a time of frustration and doubt. Ultimately, women-church desires to bring about genuinely inclusive communities of women and men in the *ecclesia* of Jesus Christ. Whether this is possible given the patriarchal and sexist history of our churches is uncertain. The extent of women's inclusion in the full life of the church will determine the development and thrust of women-church.

Women-church includes more than those who appropriate its title; it embraces those of kindred spirit, those who seek freedom from structures that keep them subservient and deny them the possibility of living according to the liberating word of a liberating God, and those who claim allegiance to a global sisterhood committed to justice for the oppressed. In that sense its membership is legion and is growing every day.

Primary Agenda

The primary agenda of women-church is not women's ordination, even though the spirit and some of the same women that birthed the Women's Ordination Conference also provided the impetus for women-church. The conviction that brought 1,600 women to Detroit in 1975 to launch a nationwide effort to open the priesthood to Roman Catholic women eventually led them to question the hierarchical, patriarchal structure of ordained ministry itself, which seems contrary to the spirit of Jesus Christ. Indeed, a significant number of Protestant women who fought so hard to achieve ordination have left their ministries, burned out by the constant struggle to overcome secondary status, overt discrimination and the pressure to succeed.

Women-church ultimately aims to humanize

Miriam Therese Winter, "The Women-Church Movement." Copyright 1989 Christian Century Foundation. Reprinted by permission from the March 8, 1989 issue of *The Christian Century*.

structures in and outside the church. This concern for justice gives Christian feminism both a social and a religious agenda. The two agendas have often coincided throughout the feminist movement. The Women's March down Fifth Avenue in New York in the summer of 1970 commemorating the 50th anniversary of the ratification of the 19th amendment granting women the right to vote was reminiscent of earlier marches of feminist suffragettes. Strangely enough, no church organization was listed among the sponsors of the 1970 event—though the first meeting of the women's suffrage movement in Seneca Falls, New York, in 1848 took place in a church, and those who launched that movement were women of the church, such as Lucretia Mott, Elizabeth Cady Stanton and Susan B. Anthony. These and the many feminist reformers who labored tirelessly for social and political freedoms were sustained in their difficult ministries through mutual support, which is the essence of women-church.

While women's liberation in America has not always maintained a religious affiliation, feminist leaders who never espoused religion, as well as those who did and then left it, are considered a part of the women-church sisterhood, and their achievements are acknowledged with satisfaction and pride. As Gloria Steinem reminded participants in Cincinnati: "We [women] are the one group that does not have a nation. We need to make a psychic country" to which all women can belong. Women-church is doing just that, recognizing in the process that its history extends well beyond the boundaries of its own rather recent beginnings.

Fear of Women's Movement

Church leaders have reason to fear the women's movement. Christian feminism has never been satisfied with a religion separated from public life, nor has it ever settled for merely incremental modifications in the religious establishment. Women-church and traditional church have contrasting understandings of God, grace and world, and of their interrelationship. True partnership and mutuality between the two forms of church will take more than a canonical pronouncement or a shift in regulations. It will require the traditional church's learning a new way of behaving. The church will have to learn how experience can be a source of grace; learn to speak less dogmatically and act less hierarchically; learn to communicate more and excommunicate less; learn to care as much about people as it does about structures and forms. In small faith-sharing circles, the Spirit of God is leading women to shape the future church of Jesus Christ.

In carving out a new tradition, women-church is laying a solid theological foundation for its claims. There has been an explosion of feminist literature in the past two dozen years that challenges age-old assumptions on every conceivable front. Feminist

philosophers, sociologists, ethicists, liturgists and those who are engaged in the arts are expanding our collective understandings of God and of ourselves.

The heart of women-church, however, is what happens in personal encounters to bring texture, color and meaning to the tangled threads of women's lives. In her autobiographical book *The Journey Is Home*, Nelle Morton describes the phenomenon of women's awakening, which is the core of feminist faith. In small, intimate gatherings, women tell their stories, moving through pain, defensiveness, anger, even rage, into an awareness that it is all right to feel the way they feel, and to be who they are. The liberating force of this realization is grace.

"Women came to new speech simply because they were being heard," Morton writes. Hearing becomes an act of receiving the woman as well as her words. In women-church women do not have to be "good" or obedient or even right. They can just be the self that God loved into being. Women-church affirms woman's reality, affirms who women are and are becoming. Women-church must emphasize this "I'm OK, you're OK" aspect as long as derogatory structures and situations continue to oppress women.

Movement of Men and Women

Associated with the women-church movement are men and many women from nearly every walk of life—a kaleidoscope of creeds, cultures, colors and classes, of extraordinary and ordinary women, our mothers, our sisters, ourselves. It includes very angry women and women of humor and hope, radical women and traditional women, even a few who are not quite sure what all the fuss is about. For some, women-church is a way to bring new energy into congregational life; for others, it offers an occasional alternative to their regular church routine; still others find it a substitute for a church commitment that has died; and some cling to it as a lifeline in turbulent times.

Women-church gives identity to sisterhood and support for women's difficult journey. It offers a setting where the reinterpretation, reinvention and re-creation of foundational myths is possible and legitimate.

"The Spirit of God is leading women to shape the future church of Jesus Christ."

The concept of women-church does have its limitations. Truly inclusive communities cannot be for women only, nor will women apart from men succeed in achieving true social and religious emancipation. Women-church must find ways to include caring men, while recognizing the need for women, and men, to seek nurture separately from time to time.

And though the women-church spirit is inclusive,

the word "church" in its name leaves out women who espouse other religious traditions; women who practice witchcraft and celebrate goddess rites; women of no particular religion and no desire to join any kind of church; and women who are connected to an inner spirit and live religiously.

"Women-church . . . means establishing bases for a feminist critical culture and celebrational community that have some autonomy from the established institutions."

At this stage, it remains unclear exactly what women-church is. Is it an ecumenical, cross-cultural, interfaith extension of the women's movement in America that cannot be understood by those church institutions it seeks to reform? Does it represent a strategy for reforming the church? Its members hold a variety of opinions about such questions, and most are more concerned about concrete issues than about theories or theology. Many would agree with Rosemary Radford Ruether's comment in *Women-Church*: "Women-church means neither leaving the church as a sectarian group, nor continuing to fit into it on its terms. It means establishing bases for a feminist critical culture and celebrational community that have some autonomy from the established institutions."

Growth is never easy, nor is it predictable. A Methodist missionary woman earlier in this century spoke words appropriate to women-church today: "Grow we must, even if we outgrow all that we love." We may outgrow forms and functions, and some cherished relationships and situations, but we will never outgrow the love of Love—only our ways of naming that Love and the rites we use to respond to the One who is Love in us.

Miriam Therese Winter is a professor of liturgy, worship, and spirituality at Hartford Seminary in Connecticut and author of WomanPrayer, WomanSong: Resources for Ritual.

"Anti-masculinity . . . now poses a serious threat to the spiritual lives of men as well as to the unity of the church."

Feminist Theology Harms Christianity

Patrick M. Arnold

The rise of the feminist movement has created a powerful and healthy movement in liberal Western Christianity that allows increasing numbers of people to liberate themselves from interiorized cultural stereotypes, repressive social roles and heretical anti-body theologians. One vibrant offspring of feminist thought is the development of "sexual spirituality," the perception that the distinctive qualities of feminine and masculine psychology influence the way we value and relate to ourselves, to each other and especially to God. These developing sexual spiritualities promise to reconcile persons to their physicality rather than alienate them from their own embodiment.

But deep below this powerful wave of feminist change, unfortunately, there flows a hidden undertow that threatens to sweep unsuspecting victims further toward a spiritual abyss of alienation from their own nature and from God. The dangerous current swirling beneath the Christian feminist movement is nothing less than a pervasive hostility to masculinity and men. Though most Christian feminists would distance themselves from this attitude as inimical to the very goals that feminism seeks to achieve, anti-masculinity prevails in so many places and at so many levels of liberal Christianity that it now poses a serious threat to the spiritual lives of men as well as to the unity of the church. Indeed, radical feminism in many ways mirrors the other end of the ideological spectrum, fundamentalism, which denigrates women, devalues the feminine and threatens Christian unity.

Hostile Attitudes

It is easy to dismiss an animosity toward maleness when it bursts out from unbalanced radical feminists who have already cut themselves off from reasonable dialogue and communion with the rest of Christianity in the formation of the schismatic "Womyn-Church."

Patrick M. Arnold, "In Search of the Hero: Masculine Spirituality and Liberal Christianity," *America*, October 7, 1989. Reprinted with permission of America Press, Inc., 106 W. 56th Street, New York, NY 10019, © 1989. All Rights Reserved.

It is more troubling—and more symptomatic of the pervasiveness of the underlying problem—when one encounters overt anti-masculine sexism in otherwise responsible male and female Christian feminists who are making salutary contributions to feminist consciousness and apt criticisms of institutional ecclesiastical oppression. Especially disturbing is the fact that many of these anti-masculine feminists have attained powerful positions in liberal Christian academia, publishing, seminary formation and parish life. A whole generation of Christian leaders is quietly and unconsciously imbibing from them subtly hostile attitudes toward men and maleness.

It is increasingly common to hear in theological discourse, classroom lectures, pastoral counseling and spiritual conversation statements to the effect that males are essentially dominating, that men are naturally violent, that masculinity is inherently patriarchal, that maleness is basically the source of all violence, that only women can be authentic Christians, that males are not naturally religious or that men are only interested in power and money. Objections to these overtly sexist remarks are sometimes dismissed with such curious justifications as: "Now you know how sexual oppression feels," or "You're a man—you can take it."

Worse, and more commonly, there *are* no objections to this theologically "justified" prejudice. At a deep level, many men unconsciously agree that they really are not very good people and that radical feminism has discovered and exposed them for the spiritually shallow and unworthy beings they really are. Other men resent these statements but keep silent because the developing feminist power centers—especially in academia—can now punish objections to radical feminist dogma with a storm of retribution that adversely affects careers—hiring, tenure and publication. Male students are increasingly vulnerable to feminist ideologization as well; for example, a field education director recently flunked a seminarian on his final examination because he responded incorrectly in a test case that unfairly forced him to choose between upholding an official church position and supporting a "correct" feminist interpretation.

New Sexual Dualism

Radical feminism is developing a new sexual Manichaeism that essentially holds that the feminine archetype equals life and nurturing while the masculine archetype equals violence and domination. This simplistic dualism identifies masculinity with its worst aspects and refuses to acknowledge its graces. No doubt this is because women have suffered so much under the "shadow" of static or rigid maleness: unbending laws, disembodied principles, unemotional judgments and oppressive violence. But men have also suffered under these things throughout history—Jesus of Nazareth among them! The inability to see that there exists also a "deep" or dynamic masculinity that can lead to extraordinary and everyday heroism constitutes a tragic and, at times, deliberate blindness to the good that lies within the hearts of men—and women as well.

Feminist Manichaeism's repression of dynamic masculinity is only an ideologically advanced form of an ancient and deep-seated hostility toward male sexuality that has plagued Western Christianity for centuries. While feminist theory has shown convincingly that what has been previously regarded as a generic animosity toward the body and sexuality in Christianity since patristic times actually masked a fear of the feminine, it fails to recognize that our spiritual history also often purveyed a deep distrust of masculine sexuality. This is not to deny the reality of historical patriarchy; the church undoubtedly fostered a dominating and rigid clerical patriarchy—but only for the benefit of those few men who were also willing to renounce sexual expressiveness and generativity. Moreover, Holy Mother Church exacted at times an even higher price from males willing to serve the church: spiritual emasculation, i.e., the abandonment of autonomy, self-expressiveness, independence and even individuation—in short, dynamic masculinity. The church was male-dominated, all right—by the very few males willing to pay a high price for power.

"Radical feminism tends also to sterilize Christianity's life-giving manliness."

This latent anti-masculinity still causes most men to remain on the fringes of Christianity. One can see them, as always, standing apart, at the back of the church—if indeed they come at all—or bored and detached amid the congregation. Many men in Western cultures simply cannot relate satisfactorily to the Christian spirituality presented to them. One way to gauge this phenomenon is to take a head count at your local church next Sunday; the female-to-male ratio will likely range between 2:1 and 5:1. The males who do attend Mass are frequently older men who have acquired wise and faithful spiritualities, men attending for the sake of family unity or young boys who have been dragged into the church most unwillingly.

Both Christian men and women have come unconsciously to believe that the church is woman's natural domain and that a man can relate to God only through women or through becoming *like* women. This attitude reinforces sexist stereotypes that women are spiritual and men worldly, women moral and men pragmatic, women nurturing and men violent. Unfortunately, elements in the liberal church are now raising this sexist prejudice to the level of an explicit ideology in theological schools where the women and men who will minister to our young people, preach our sermons, counsel our marriages, give our retreats and write our books and articles are taught to eschew everything that smacks of masculinity. There the dwindling numbers of male seminarians are occasionally berated for their "chauvinism" in moving toward ministry, picketed at their ordinations, instructed to avoid masculine metaphors for God, taught to shun words like "Father," "Lord" and "Son," encouraged to suspect biblical passages of patriarchal bias and asked to regard their entire spiritual tradition as alienating and offensive to women.

Projecting Negative Characteristics

One effect of radical feminist sexual Manichaeism is unconsciously to project negative characteristics, such as the will to power, on all men—or at least on the nearest convenient man. This tendency can create glaring contradictions in feminist theological rhetoric: though it espouses values like nurturing and life giving, for example, the rhetorical goal is inevitably to wrest *power* from "power-hungry" men. With projection comes denial. As extreme feminists fasten exclusively on the real evils that men do, it is virtually unheard of for them to question whether a "shadow" side of femininity might exist that needs to be examined. Could a distinctively feminine "violence" exist? And could two million abortions every year in the United States have anything to do with it?

As the feminist movement exorcises from Christianity the demons of patriarchy, it threatens to cast out powerful angels of masculinity as well; in sanitizing the tradition of machismo, radical feminism tends also to sterilize Christianity's life-giving manliness. Obedient to its ideological dictates, the resulting self-deprecating, docile "feminist men" grow perceptibly alienated from their ancient masculine roots, estranged from their myths and separated from the images, metaphors and rituals that can lead them to spiritual depth. Their God, victim of a sex-change, loves no longer as a father, but as an abstract and neutered "warm fuzzy." Their Jesus, once again meek and mild, no longer calls them to radical discipleship and the cross but only to nurturing and gentleness. Their liturgy, once a powerhouse of transformational symbols, often degenerates into a butterfly-banner-and-balloon affair with much fussing and fluttering about. Even the last vestiges of the manhood initiation rite, the confirmation slap, disappeared without a whimper.

Spiritual Emasculation

What happens to men divorced from a deep spiritual experience of their own manhood? Two kinds of tragedy. For those suffering spiritual emasculation, it is a failure of energy. Poet Robert Bly once described feminized men as unhappy, lacking in energy and "life-preserving, but not exactly *life-giving*." After the necessary task of "getting in touch with" their feminine side, many of these men unconsciously have chosen to remain there, trapped in the narcissism of domesticity: the "negative feminine." Fortunately, male myth, story and ritual are all about yielding male spiritual *energy*, a quality once described by Bly as the "wild man" or by Walter Ong, S.J., as "fighting for life." Newly neutered Christianity is beginning to produce a generation of men with no "wildness" and no "fight" in them, a blow-dried, Gucci-shoed and sun-tanned lot whose primary moral achievement is "being nice." How chauvinistically scandalous and antiquated the famous prayer of St. Ignatius now must sound to them: "To give and not count the cost, to fight and not heed the wounds, to toil and not seek for rest, to labor and not seek for reward, save that of knowing we are doing Your most holy will."

For many other men, the lack of an attractive male spirituality leads to more tragic results. Confronted with a religion that seems to require that they abandon and repent of their male qualities and that provides more moral reprobation than spiritual guidance, many men unhesitatingly choose to fight for money, careers or power. And major corporations ("Dow lets you do great things") or the military ("Be all that you can be") are all too ready to exploit their deepest masculine desires. The result is usually vicious competitiveness and an unrestrained "agonism" that lets loose the worst demons inside men and wounds anyone unfortunate enough to stand in their way. But the price of unspiritual masculine stress is ultimately devastating to the men themselves, as Jan Harper has suggested in the title of her study of "successful" businessmen, *Quiet Desperation*. Other measures of the cost of unbalanced masculinity are even more appalling: a suicide rate 300 percent that of women; a life expectancy 10 years less than women's; nine times as many men in prison; higher rates of male alcohol and drug abuse, and higher rates of victimization from murder, assault and major disease than women.

The consequences of emasculated Christianity are even more apparent in the state of modern male youth. Since it has become unfashionable in liberal Christianity "to be a man," our culture no longer provides the wise stories, rites and rituals that once marked the passage of boys to adulthood. The result is that many of our boys are becoming not men, but sociopathic monsters. When Joseph Campbell was asked what the results of the disappearance of male adult initiation rites was, he replied simply: "Read today's New York Times." Outbreaks such as the murderous "wilding" spree in Central Park have many complex causes, but the lack of a forceful initiation of young boys into a vivid experience of male adulthood as an ordeal of service for the people is certainly among them.

"Christian men need . . . liberation from the pervasive and disabling liberal Western notion that religion is basically a feminine phenomenon."

Christian men urgently need to rediscover a life-giving masculine spirituality. But they first need liberation from the pervasive and disabling liberal Western notion that religion is basically a feminine phenomenon. An imaginary trip around the world might quickly shatter that idea. Listen to Buddhist monks in Tibet as they shake their monastery with the deep-throated *aum*. Witness throngs of Hindu men making their annual pilgrimage to Benares. Watch a sea of Muslim males pray passionately to Allah in a huge Arabian mosque. Join Hasidic men in Jerusalem as they *doven* earnestly in prayer at the Western Wall. See the joyous faces of African tribesmen, scarred with ritual signs of their manhood. Pray with Mexican *penitentes* as they approach Guadalupe on their knees. Sweat in a South Dakota *initipi* ("life-lodge") as holy men fast and pray in the Lakota fashion. Or, for that matter, join charismatic evangelicals at a local businessmen's prayer breakfast. Everywhere around the world, at this moment, a billion men are seeking their God, fasting for visions, expiating their sins, singing divine praises and enduring hardships for faith and justice. Men are naturally deeply religious, all right; it is just that our modern culture provides little help for them anymore in finding their natural masculine spirituality.

The Hero Motif

How can modern Christian men find this source again? Fortunately, the way to masculine spirituality is still open to those willing to search, and though there may be little guidance for this journey at the moment, the rewards of making it are rich. One place to start is libraries or bookstores (some of which are just now beginning to sprout tiny "men's studies" shelves) where there lies a vast treasury of male myths, images and stories.

> *"Our ministers must learn to speak to alienated men in a language that they can understand, rather than a rhetoric that puts them down."*

One might explore a classic like Joseph Campbell's *The Hero with a Thousand Faces,* which identified the fundamental myth of the hero as a recurring motif in world literature, ritual, symbol and even psychology. Campbell discovered a pattern of heroic behavior that is key to masculine spiritual development: the need to separate and depart from the safe and familiar, to undergo ordeals in search of a boon or benefit and to return home with new-found empowerment on behalf of the people.

Understanding Maleness

Men can also understand maleness through empathetic sensitivity to the sheer animality of kindred males in nature and find embarrassingly and humorously reflected in their animal relatives the basic hormone-driven qualities that so influence their own human hearts: cockiness, prickliness, colorful beauty, majestic bearing, territoriality, sexual heat, protectiveness. But men may learn best about masculinity from the company of other men. They experience there the obvious things: bravado, aggressiveness, competition, ribald humor, braggadocio. But if they are lucky, and travel in the right circles, they will learn much more: about quiet strength, keeping their word, respecting the law, thinking for themselves, sticking to their guns, standing for principle, watching out for the "little guy," respecting women and laughing at themselves. All of these virtues are high on the list of male values. Fortunately, a small Christian "men's movement" has also begun to provide guided workshops that facilitate such encounters at such centers as the Center for Action and Contemplation in Albuquerque, N.M., under the direction of Richard Rohr, O.F.M.

Yet at the deepest level, the discovery of masculinity must include actual experience, for masculinity is finally not something observed, not something imagined or read about, but something *done*; not a virtue given in nature, but a capability achieved through risk. It means actually undertaking the hero journey: leaving the safe comforts of home for an adventurous exploration of the world—and the self. It demands an ordeal—a struggle with demons and dragons real and imagined. And it requires, finally, a return—to a life of service and responsibility on behalf of the people. Masculinity is all about heroic suffering, not for its own sake, but to provide good things for a family, a nation, a church.

Only when a man actually "follows his bliss" and responds to his own unique call to heroism can he understand masculinity. Such a journey may lead to an intimidating medical school and a healing career, bring him to fight society's callousness on behalf of the homeless, or draw him into a foxhole to defend his country against foreign attack. He might also find the now scandalous interior archetype of "warrior" by fighting forest fires in Montana and AIDS in a San Francisco laboratory. Perhaps he might live out the role of "patriarch"—by wisely guiding his family to growth and success. Or perhaps he will find in himself a clown, an artist, a prophet or even a priest. In all of these experiences and a million more, a man can find his masculinity etched deeply into every cell of his body and every secret niche of his psyche.

The question is, will the Christian church help—or hinder—this journey? Our theologians, teachers, pastors and spiritual care-givers must wake up to the liberal church's inattentiveness and even hostility to explicitly male spiritual needs. Our spiritual counselors must begin to understand empathetically "what makes men tick," rather than use them for ideological target practice. Our liturgists must recreate the kinds of community initiation rites into manhood that once celebrated a boy's crossover to full social responsibility. Our ministers must learn to speak to alienated men in a language that they can understand, rather than a rhetoric that puts them down. We must encourage men as well as women to celebrate their own sexuality.

Navigating the Extremes

Perhaps the church can one day successfully navigate between the Scylla of fundamentalism and the Charybdis of radical feminism so that women can emerge to full ministerial empowerment and unquestioned ecclesiastical status while men find their own heroic roles in service to the Christian community without having to apologize for or repress their native dynamic spirituality. Perhaps on that day we can truly appreciate each individual for his or her special and unique gifts, granted through the miracle of sexuality.

Patrick M. Arnold is an assistant professor of Old Testament at the University of San Diego. He is writing a book on biblical literature and men's religious values.

*"The issue of women priests is one . . .
that indicate[s] a deep-seated lack of
respect for women in our church."*

viewpoint 20

Women Should Be Included in the Priesthood

Joan Garvey Hermes

Item: Our son makes his debut as an altar boy. I am moved as I watch him participate in this ritual that my brothers and his father were part of many years ago. But something is missing.

Item: A beloved uncle, a priest, dies. His funeral is a testament to his 30 years of ministry to his parish. More than 90 of his brother priests concelebrate his funeral Mass. But something is missing.

Item: It is Vocation Sunday in my family's parish. An appealing young priest reassures the congregation that the diminishing numbers of priests and nuns should not be alarming but rather a reminder that Catholics are returning to a church tradition of fuller participation by the laity in the work of the church. But something is missing.

Ours is an open family. We find it easy to talk with our children. When questions about sex, drugs, or puzzling current events come up, we are at ease with explanations and feelings. But the question of why there are no women priests stops us in our tracks; and I, for one, find myself slow to come up with answers or explanations that address this painful issue.

Five of our six children are girls. They are born feminists. Two of their favorite baby-sitters, both young women, are now a doctor and a lawyer. My best friend from college, who is a woman, is a successful attorney. Their uncle is a husband, father, and a nurse. These, then, are girls who have grown up in a world where women are encouraged to set high goals and pursue them. The notion that sex does not define vocational possibilities is a given. So how do I respond when they ask why their church refuses to consider female candidates for the priesthood?

I find it easy to talk about the political and spiritual church. I tell them that, in my opinion, it is the political church that has taken an outdated tradition and held to it as if it were gospel truth. We talk about

God the creator and the fact that we can be certain that God, in creating men and women in his image and likeness, created them equally. We talk about Jesus and his life on earth. We talk of Veronica and her courage in a hostile crowd; Martha and Mary, two opposites that Jesus treasured as friends. I tell our girls that I think the Holy Spirit chose these stories and others like them to be part of the Gospel to say that Jesus did not consider women to be second-class citizens and that his choice of men to be his Apostles might have been, as was his incarnation in male form, an adaptation to the times in which he chose to come to earth. In short, then, when I talk about the unfortunate oxymoron, women priests, I try to teach that God is not part of this human error.

Flawed Church

But here is the difficult part. I feel that the issue of women priests is one of several issues, a celibate clergy is another, that indicate a deep-seated lack of respect for women in our church. I understand that there are wonderful men in the church who would tell me that this position is incorrect, but this feeling on my part runs deep. How do I explain this to young people and, at the same time, encourage them to love and be loyal to a flawed church?

I am angry that a group of men, a "good ol' boys" network if you will, can deny to half the world's population the possibility of serving God and others through the priesthood. If my children watch newsreel footage that shows Southern sheriffs with firehoses turning back black marchers, I know what to say: this is wrong; this is evil. Period. It's not so easy to talk about the injustice of sexism when the firehoses can't be seen. But we do talk. And I try to express my own confusion at finding the balance between forgiveness and refusal to accept injustice, even though those acting unjustly may be well-meaning people.

I am a feminist. But I am also a Catholic.

Joan Garvey Hermes, "Mom, Why Can't Girls Be Priests?" *U.S. Catholic,*
August 1989. Reprinted with permission from *U.S. Catholic,* published by
Claretian Publications, 205 W. Monroe, Chicago, IL 60606.

Sometimes these two beliefs bump into one another. The Catholic Church's stand on birth control, for example, is, in the world's eyes, antifeminist. Yet while it may not be easy for some to agree with, I believe that the approach we are encouraged and taught to take is motivated by compassion and the notion of openness to the will of God. I believe that life begins at conception, and I find the church's stand on abortion a reasonable one. But, try as I might, I find nothing in the concept of an all-male clergy worth supporting. I see nothing in it of God's will. I feel bound to express this to my children.

When our older children study the bishops' letters on social-justice issues, I am proud that they are part of a church that continues to grow in the notion that it is through addressing social issues that we teach as Jesus taught and strive to do his work on earth. But I also draw their attention to my feeling that the bishops are late in struggling with the social-justice issue so central to the issue of women as priests.

Women and the Priesthood

I worry when I talk to our children of my feelings about women and the priesthood. It is with this issue that I feel most ill at ease in my parental role. Because it is here that I must look at my own participation in the Catholic Church. It is here that I must work out the dilemma faced by so many my age who want to say yes to their church yet feel that some of its flaws are, ironically, unchristian.

I am angry at a situation that seems unlikely to change within my lifetime. I worry about the bitterness this can inspire. I worry even more about being called to believe in a church leader who seems to be working to move the church that I love back to an age where things on the surface were much easier. And much less challenging. Those of us who have seen it both ways, we pre- and post-Vatican II Catholics, cannot and do not choose to return to those times.

I want each of our six children to feel that God is central in their lives. I want all their decisions about vocations to be based on a desire to serve God. I want them to ask God's help in making these decisions.

I have made my choice of vocation. As my children begin to make their own choices, I need to be more honest with myself about the issue of women priests. I need to be more open with them about my own confusion on this issue. And I need to find a way to encourage them to, literally, keep the faith in the face of this challenge to their participation in the Catholic Church. Perhaps forgiveness is the key. I do feel bound to tell them that forgiveness, rather than acceptance, is called for.

Encourage Action

Item: While our parish has no altar girls, we have been in parishes that do. When our next daughter reaches fifth grade and the all-boy training program for servers begins, we will ask how she feels about this. We will encourage less acceptance and more action.

"I find nothing in the concept of an all-male clergy worth supporting. I see nothing in it of God's will."

Item: While the beauty of those many fellow-priests concelebrating my uncle's funeral Mass was moving, my children were privileged to see another form of witness. A family friend, also a priest, was not present on the altar. Because he disagrees with the church's position on women and the priesthood, this man chose to worship in the congregation, dressed in his black clerical suit. I am grateful for this. May we see more like him.

Item: As the numbers of priests diminish, I pray that the Catholic Church will be moved to see women differently. During World War II the numbers of men in industry decreased and women took their places. The world changed. And continues to change. Perhaps one Vocation Sunday I will see a young priest speaking dressed in her best black dress.

When my eldest daughter was in fifth grade, she signed up for intramural basketball. This had been a boys-only sport at her grade school. When she was told that girls didn't play intramural basketball, she gathered together enough of her friends so that they were strong enough in number to go to the principal and say "they do now." For years now this grade school has had co-ed intramural sports.

If one of our girls should feel a genuine calling to serve God as a priest, my husband and I would hope she could join with a group of like-minded women to say "they do now." And then we would watch and pray.

Joan Garvey Hermes is a free-lance writer living in Bourbonnais, Illinois.

"Jesus was born and died a male, so those who take his part in the drama of the eucharist must also be male."

viewpoint 21

Women Should Be Excluded from the Priesthood

Elden Curtiss

Could the role of Hamlet in Shakespeare's famous drama be portrayed adequately by a woman as a woman? Only if the plot were rewritten and the relationships and dialogue of the main characters substantially changed, but then it would not be the work of Shakespeare.

Could the role of Jesus in the re-presentation of the paschal mysteries in the eucharistic liturgy be portrayed adequately by a woman as a woman? Only if the plot were rewritten and the relationships and dialogue changed, but then it would not be the Father's work as we have received it in our tradition.

It seems to me that the Vatican Congregation for the Doctrine of the Faith (Declaration on the Question of the Admission of Women to the Ministerial Priesthood, 1976) made an essential point in maintaining that only an ordained male priest can take the part of Jesus in the specific cultic role of celebrating the eucharistic sacrifice. The plan of God is revealed to us in the words and actions of Jesus and the interpretation of the early church and the subsequent development of our tradition. The teaching authority of the church does not believe that the plan of God as revealed in the development of the sacrament of orders was simply culturally conditioned in favor of males, but that as Jesus was born and died a male, so those who take his part in the drama of the eucharist must also be male.

Although it is the resurrected Christ who lives in our midst, and all of us, male and female, share in his new life, which transcends all human conditions and limitations, the eucharistic sacrifice makes present to us the reality of the crucifixion of Jesus as it touches our lives. It is precisely in this re-presentation of the suffering and death of Jesus as a man that the ordained priest must be able to portray him in his total human dimension. . . .

The traditional requirement that only an ordained male priest can celebrate the eucharist is not, therefore, a matter of discrimination against women. It flows from the natural distinction between male and female. Because Jesus is a male in his human existence, his life and death are re-presented by a male priest.

The specific cultic role of the ordained priest has nothing to do with the equality of membership in the church or the common priesthood of the people of God that is ours by baptism. It has nothing to do with the call to ministry which is given to all the members of the church through the Spirit or the developing ministries in the church shared by women and men.

The sacrament of orders is meant to be a sacrament of ministerial service to all the baptized, to all the other ministries. It is meant to be the special support ministry for everyone in the church. It is not meant to replace all the ministries of the people or to neglect or, even worse, to suppress them. The ordained priesthood is meant to be a coordinating ministry, guided by collaborative and consultative processes, which enables the ministry of all the people of God to have cohesion and direction for the building up of the entire church.

Reasons for Tension and Concern

When American women feel excluded from significant roles in the church and from responsible ministry; when their gifts and charisms are not fully appreciated or accepted or utilized; when they experience powerlessness in terms of planning and decision making and evaluation, then it is no wonder that some pressure to be numbered among those who manage the resources and make the decisions.

When total control of the church is perceived or experienced to be in clerical hands alone; when there are no real dialogical or consultative processes in the parish or larger diocesan church; when the ministry of women seems only to be tolerated or even

Elden Curtiss, "Maleness and the Priest's Cultic Role," *Origins,* December 21, 1989.

male/female roles   77

discouraged when it reaches a certain administrative level, then the issues about the ordination of women to priesthood and episcopacy are raised because they seem the only way to authority and power in the church.

And when women of faith accept the centrality of the eucharist in the life of the church, they rightfully are concerned about the diminishing number of priests throughout our country. They realize that the church may experience a gradual shift in emphasis and practice from eucharistic celebrations to liturgies of the word only. If there are not enough men who are willing to be priests in the future, what will happen to the essential liturgical and sacramental life of the church?

It is important for us to separate the ecclesial issues about discipleship and management and statistics in the church from the cultic role of the ordained priesthood. They affect each other, but they are not the same.

Cultic Role of Priests

We believe that in the eucharistic sacrifice Jesus is re-presented to his people as priest and victim through the cultic role of the ordained priest. Jesus chose the Twelve Apostles from among his disciples to be representative of the 12 tribes of Israel in order to indicate the continuity of God's ancient covenant with his people. These apostles became the foundation of the ordained priesthood in the church. At the Last Supper, they and their successors are commanded by the Lord to continue the re-presentation of the paschal mysteries by which they and their people are to be saved.

"The priesthood of Jesus would be exercised . . . [by] men like himself . . . because they would be clear signs of his sacrificial death as a man."

There is to be a continuity of sacrifice in the new covenant, but instead of the blood of animals, the blood of the Lamb of God becomes the one, perpetual offering until the end of time. Jesus will continue to be the priest and victim through his apostles, and the sacrifice will be re-enacted and re-presented every time the eucharist is celebrated in the world. This is the specific cultic role of ordained priests, to act in the person of Christ (*in persona Christi*), so that his human life and death are remembered and re-experienced through their words and actions, which are his.

Just as there were men, priests of the tribe of Levi, who were specially deputized to offer sacrifice under the former covenant, so Jesus willed to continue the use of sacrifice as the primary way to worship God, but now with the perfect offering of himself through the men he specially deputized to offer this sacrifice. Because they take his place and are the visible and audible human signs of his suffering and death as a man—"this is *my body* which will be given up for you"—they are to be men like himself. This tradition of ordaining only males to the priesthood is rooted in the words and actions of Jesus, and the history of Israel, and the interpretation of the early church and the practice of the church through the centuries.

The Ordination of Women

It seems to me, therefore, that the main problem for those who maintain that women should be ordained to priesthood—that there are no insurmountable obstacles—is that the cultic role of the ordained priest, to stand as a man in the place of Jesus the man in the re-presentation of his paschal mysteries, loses its clear sign value and historical meaning. The developing emphases since the Second Vatican Council on the eucharist as a communal meal in which all participate and the expanded role of the assembly in celebrating together the eucharist (and these are important elements long neglected in the eucharistic celebration) cannot be used to de-emphasize the essential nature of the eucharist as sacrifice and the essential role of the ordained priest to re-present Jesus in the sacred drama (cf. Letter to the Bishops of the Catholic Church on Certain Questions Concerning the Minister of the Eucharist, 1983, by the Congregation for the Doctrine of the Faith).

There can be no eucharistic sacrifice without the ministry of an ordained priest, who takes the part of Jesus in re-presenting his suffering and death and resurrection as a man.

This is the main problem with the U.S. Episcopal Church's decision to ordain women as priests and now a woman as a bishop. It is a failure to recognize the essential nature of the eucharist as sacrifice despite official documents to the contrary (such as The Final Report, Anglican-Roman Catholic International Commission, Eucharistic Doctrine, 1971—Windsor, 1981) and the consequent role of the ordained priest in taking the place of Jesus in the eucharistic sacrifice. This has led to a confusion of the common priesthood of all the baptized with the ordained priesthood, which includes the specific cultic role of re-presenting Jesus in his paschal mysteries. When the issue is one of equality before the Lord, there is no argument against the ordination of women. But when the issue becomes the specific cultic role of the ordained priest, then our Catholic tradition stands against the possibility of a woman portraying the role of Jesus, who saves us in his humanity as a male.

Magisterial Teaching

The magisterium of the church (the bishops of the world in union with the pope) does not accept the argument that the only reason Jesus chose men to be apostles was because of the patriarchal society in which he lived, that women would never have been accepted as his representatives and as leaders of men. Jesus clearly departed from cultural restraints in the way he related to women and accepted them into his community of disciples. He understood the long history of sacrifice as an essential element in Jewish worship and the tradition of the male priesthood, which was culturally conditioned. He knew that it was his Father's plan to continue the sacrificial nature of worship through the suffering and death of his Son. The priesthood of Jesus would be exercised through the apostles and their successors, men like himself, not because of cultural necessity, but because they would be clear signs of his sacrificial death as a man. The one sacrifice of Jesus on the cross is re-presented in its total reality every time the eucharist is celebrated in the world.

This is the reason that the magisterium of the church also rejects the position that there are no convincing theological arguments for limiting priestly ordination to men. This would mean that the church would have to abandon a tradition founded in the actions of Jesus—his own decision—which is based on the reality that in his humanity he is a man and that he selected certain men to take part in the re-presentation of his suffering and death as a man. But this is essential theology of the eucharist and the basis for the tradition of the ordained priesthood.

Catholic tradition cannot be understood in such a dynamic and fluid sense that, in the divine plan, the church is considered a developing mystery led by the Spirit so that what it is to be is not yet completely known, if its gradual development in response to cultural conditioning radically changes the theological or historical bases for the tradition in its origin. All tradition in the church which is recognizable as part of God's revelation to his people must be able to be directly related to its roots, to the fonts of faith.

Christian Anthropology

And, finally, it seems to me that Christian anthropology is able to help us better understand and accept the appropriateness of men in the distinctive cultic priestly role.

We recognize that our understanding of God is analogical, based on our human experience of creation, which is the effect of God's will and power, but separate from him. God is mystery beyond all human comprehension. We can only speak of him and his attributes and his revelation to us with analogies drawn from our limited observations and experiences and our analysis of creation as it relates to the Creator. Our understanding of Jesus in his relationship with Yahweh is always analogical.

In our human experience, the dynamic power of generating the life force outside of himself is the male imperative, as the dynamic power of generating the life force within herself is the female imperative.

Jesus as messiah and priest and sanctifier generated outside of himself a special life force to others. This is the reason, from our human perspective, that he was born a male. This is the reason that he always spoke of God as "Father," the One who is the source of all life and the transmitter of all life force outside of himself, out of love. And this is the reason that Jesus chose other men to be the human signs of his continuing generative role in the eucharistic sacrifice.

The cultic role of the ordained priest is to stand in the place of Jesus in the eucharistic celebration so that he might share with his people, through his sacrificial death, the special life force of the Father, which is a share in the divine life.

> "Jesus chose other men to be the human signs of his continuing generative role in the eucharistic sacrifice."

However, for all of us who are struggling to be church together, our model is a woman rather than a man. Mary's unique role was to accept the generation of divine life from God through the action of the Holy Spirit and to add the component of her human life, so that the Promised One could be incarnate. And this is the role of the church today, all of us together trying to be open to this divine life (grace), allowing it to develop within us, adding our own humanness to that divine element and then bursting forth with new life. This is the reason that the church has always been called "mother," the willing recipient and nurturer of divine life, combining with it the gift of human life which gives birth to new members in the life of the Spirit.

Male and female are the two dynamic components of all human life, and they are analogically the basic dynamics of the church in its relationship to God. It is important not only for us to acknowledge the essential difference between them, but at the same time to recognize and celebrate their inner connectedness and inner dependency in order for the church to achieve its full potential as the bride of Christ.

A New Partnership

We must develop in the church a new partnership between men and women which recognizes our anthropological differences and our human solidarity and our commonality in faith based on our mutual complementarity in living and sharing the new life that is ours from the Lord. We need to encourage and support the ministries which flow from our baptism and our confirmation with the gifts of the Spirit. We must strive to involve women and men in collaborative and consultative processes in our parishes and dioceses so that discrimination of every kind is eliminated from the life of the church at all levels.

And we need to understand and appreciate the ordained priesthood as we understand and treasure the continuing celebration of the paschal mysteries of Jesus in the eucharist. We need to analyze dispassionately the reasons why Jesus selected only men as apostles and the reasons the church has continued this tradition and must continue it in the future. We need to rejoice in the maleness of Jesus and the female dimensions of the church. And all of us who are the church must stand ready like Mary to receive the gift of divine life from God, to nurture it and give it human life and form so that it can be shared with other human beings.

"Without our male priests, the sign value of the generative ministry of Jesus to us would be inadequate."

Women have a special role in this process of giving human form and meaning to the divine life we receive. Without their dynamic power of generating new life within themselves, the effectiveness of the cultic priestly role would be diffused and dissipated.

But without our male priests, the sign value of the generative ministry of Jesus to us would be inadequate. We need this analogy of the human life process in order to better understand the reality of the suffering and death of Jesus as a man, made present to us in the eucharistic sacrifice, and the reality of the life force which the Father shares with us through the humanity of his Son.

We need active, faith-filled women in the church and in the ministries of the church, just as we need active, faith-filled men. And we need an adequate number of qualified men ordained to the ministerial priesthood so that we may be able to celebrate, everywhere the people of the church gather, the paschal mysteries of Jesus made present for us in the eucharist. These elements of church life and ministry, in their mutual dependency and complementarity, are the cause for our growing vitality as church and our future strength.

We together, then, are the church, men and women, priests and people, in our distinctive but mutual roles, who provide, with the Lord, the generative elements which give life to the church. Confusion of these roles is not the answer to the quest for equality, but complementarity and mutual respect and love and the willingness to chart a course together and to share the burdens of ministry and management in our church.

Bishop Elden Curtiss of Helena, Montana, was ordained in 1958 and has been a bishop since 1976.

"The military does not belong to men. It belongs to the citizens of the country, over half of whom are women."

The Military Should Employ More Women

Judith Hicks Stiehm

There are now more than 200,000 women in uniform. These semipermanent, minority invaders of a male institution fill a variety of nontraditional jobs—jobs that are not so dominated by women in the civilian sector that the military *must* recruit women or leave the jobs unfilled (as would be the case, for instance, with nursing). Even if these women continue to be seen as substitutes for unavailable men—that is, as "better-than-nothings"—in today's military they are substitutes not for men who have been sent to the front, but for men who have chosen to remain at home. If mobilization and/or a draft should occur, a cadre of senior, trained, professional women will already be in place—something that has never been true before.

Perhaps most important, though, women who wear uniforms are counterexamples: living disproof of widely held (and perhaps essential) beliefs about the military. An impulse to minimize the resulting dissonance would explain the recurring attempts to minimize the number of military women and the roles they play. That is, the need to minimize evidence counter to central military beliefs, rather than any objective need, may account for the military's uneasy accommodation of its token women. . . .

One [belief] is that war is manly. The second is that protectors protect. The third is that any soldier is substitutable for any other. These beliefs are widely shared, deeply held, and greatly resistant to disproof or "demythologizing." This suggests that they are functional even if not logical. People *want* to believe them.

So what? What does this knowledge contribute to our understanding of our most lethal institution? What does it mean for policymaking?

First, planners should consider "normalizing" the military: bringing the ratio of women up to the 40 to 60 percent range. Second, they should think about reserving the slots now open to women for women, instead of trying to guarantee equal access to these while reserving other slots for men only. This would guarantee more overall equity and permit a fuller utilization of talent. Third, they should consider giving women their own functional corps. Essentially this occurs with nursing now. But why not give women tanks, missiles, and supplies as well? Or give women the Air Force. Women are now eligible for most Air Force slots—just add the opportunity to fly in combat and let women have that service *in toto*. . . .

Enlisting Women

Even under existing policies, U.S. Air Force enlisted personnel could be mostly women. The modest recruitment goals now set for women are attributed to their lack of interest and qualifications. One might conclude that if large numbers of interested and qualified women suddenly sought to join the Air Force, the number of female airmen would increase and debate cease. This might not be the case. Even though Air Force women's attrition, retention, and promotion statistics are similar to those for men, many commanders continue to perceive women as a problem.

Pregnancy is described as a problem; so are single military members with dependent children or parents and married military couples. Other questions are raised about women's stamina (in addition to their strength), their ability to lead, their availability for assignment, and the effect they have on male cohesion and morale. Other questions are cast in economic terms—for example, increased costs for medical care. Yet men cost more to recruit and have more dependents and higher retirement costs. Moreover, the nation's defense involves other and more fundamental concerns than economy, including certainty of success and public support for the military.

Excerpted, with permission, from *Arms and the Enlisted Woman* by Judith Hicks Stiehm. Philadelphia: Temple University Press, 1989.

It is worth repeating that no enlisted jobs are allocated to women formally or informally. No effort is made to maximize the use of women. It is almost as though military leaders think of the services as belonging to men, who "use" some women when convenient. The military does not belong to men. It belongs to the citizens of the country, over half of whom are women. The military is a national institution intended to protect all citizens. It is under, and not apart from, government; it is not a vehicle for the aggrandizement of individuals. It is a burden to the country, and those who participate in it serve their fellow citizens and take direction from an elected commander in chief.

" 'Discrimination' occurs now because equipment is designed so that more men can use it than women."

Men who command should not think of women's participation in the military as just a matter of emergency "use." Instead, the whole population of young people should be considered potentially available to serve the nation—and not just in a particular service, but in the services as a whole. If service is thought of in this way, the assignment of "less-usable" individuals to reserved slots because they are the only slots those individuals can fill might make sense.

For example, if the Air Force needs 300 speakers of French, it assigns French-speaking enlistees to slots requiring French even if those individuals prefer other slots. English-speaking-only positions are, in essence, reserved for the English-speaking-only. Similarly, if certain jobs require men for combat, physical strength, and mechanical knowledge, men are assigned to them even if they would prefer office jobs. And shouldn't the only jobs women *can* qualify for be reserved for them in order to use them? Why shouldn't women predominate in the jobs that are available to them and for which they qualify, even if men can also do them and want them—especially if the men are needed elsewhere?

Concern for the Men

The 88 percent male Air Force is concerned that it is discriminating against men. But even if women were to get more than half the jobs for which both men and women are eligible, and even if women were to get them when there were eligible men who wanted them, men would not necessarily be discriminated against. As long as only men can be used in certain crucial jobs, a "pull" to an area of need, rather than a barrier to an area of preference, cannot be considered discrimination. Some other "discrimination" occurs now because equipment is

designed so that more men can use it than women. This means that men are siphoned off to tasks that they might not prefer, leaving a reduced number of men to compete with all women.

The Air Force's stated reverence for the existing propensities of young people and its lack of interest in affecting existing predispositions are hard to take seriously. The best utilization of the country's human resources may be quite different from its past utilization when the services' needs and citizens' needs for participation are fully considered. Congressman Les Aspin (D.-Wisc.), who became chair of the House Armed Services Committee in 1985, was chair of the Subcommittee on Military Personnel and Compensation in 1984. . . . He concluded that "the service that at first blush appeared to have the best record of utilizing women suddenly turns out to have the worst record." Even if one accepts the combat exclusion as a given, Aspin noted, the Army was filling 22 percent of jobs open to women with women, the Navy 23 percent, the Marines 30 percent, and the Air Force only 12 percent. Aspin's committee therefore recommended that the Air Force be directed to recruit more women (up to 25 percent of recruits by 1987), thus increasing its use of women and decreasing its use of men, who might then become available to the other services.

The Air Force Disagrees

Tydal McCoy, assistant secretary of the Air Force for manpower, reserve affairs and installation, found Aspin's arguments "superficial" and asserted that the level of female Air Force recruits under the Carter administration (20 percent) was "artificially high" and "actually lowered women's status in the service." Moreover, he argued, mandated female quotas would "discriminate against males who might consider military careers" but would be forced aside. Air Force concern about discrimination against men extended even to "gender oriented recruitment," which it forbade. McCoy concluded that increasing female accessions from 15 to 22 percent would lower Air Force productivity, increase its accession and training costs, exacerbate attrition, and "hurt" enlisted women. Meanwhile, the Air Force opened some of the few remaining fields then closed to women, including the long-debated position of security specialist. (This change opened 26,000 of the 60,000 previously closed jobs.)

Aspin prevailed. The Fiscal Year 1985 Defense Authorization Bill required the Air Force to make women 19 percent of recruits by the end of Fiscal Year 1987 and 22 percent by 1988. It also directed the Air Force to (1) determine its actual ability to utilize women, and (2) replace its accession methodology with one based on "capacity" or "demand." McCoy continued to resist, describing the mandated change as "micro management" and warning that it would force "certain inefficiencies" not in the best interest of the United States. "We're doing our own study of women," he said: ". . . we'll be looking into what kinds of jobs could be suitable and proper for women. Once we're finished, Congress may want to reconsider.". . .

The Threat of Women

When he retired as chairman of the Joint Chiefs of Staff in 1984, Gen. John W. Vessey, Jr., said, "The greatest change that has come about in the United States Forces in the time I've been in the military service has been the extensive use of women. . . . That is even greater than nuclear weapons, I feel, as far as our own forces are concerned."

Is this credible? Can a handful of young, unprivileged women be more unsettling than nuclear arms? . . . Enlisted women are ordinary women, most of whom are just trying to do their job—with dignity. Few of them wish to change the world, and fewer of them think they are doing so. Enlisted women, then, have more in common with Rosa Parks than with Susan B. Anthony. Yet, merely by insisting upon their own validity and impinging on men's consciousness, they create disarray in the world's mightiest military organization. . . .

Enlisted women serve in four services, in many countries, in hundreds of jobs, and under thousands of commanders, who have a substantial amount of discretionary power. Enlisted women's culture is multiracial, but it is relatively homogeneous with regard to education and social class, and it is very age-stratified. Women who enlist make a nontraditional decision. Once in service, though, they encounter the men in our culture who are most devoted to polarized roles for women and men.

"The military's role as a social institution should be recognized, and just as young men are trained and prepared for work in civilian life, young women could be supported as mothers."

Moreover, since sex integration, these very men have had to lead and command women, including lesbian women. Having to police woman-to-woman relationships has been difficult for some men, and their discomfort may have had the effect of driving what were previously (tacitly) accepted relationships into the closet, and of disrupting the bonds between straight women and straight and lesbian women. Thus, integration has probably affected the bonds between women as much as it is said to have affected those between men, yet as the military integrated, it did little (at least self-consciously) either to assess this loss or to foster male-female bonding in the enterprise

known as "soldiering.". . .

If one assumes that women are as competent as men to serve in their nation's defense, and that as citizens they are equally obliged to do so, and if one also assumes that the nation can and should be militarily defended, one must conclude that current policies do not make much sense. The tedious sifting of the military's own documents, rationales, and evidence leads to this conclusion. . . . The Navy's discomfort with women on ships, the disjunction between Army research findings and the policies pushed by commanders, and the elaborate formulas created by the Air Force for women's accessions suggest that defensiveness rather than sense drives much of the policy on women.

A great deal of military time and effort has been consumed by women's issues during the last fifteen years. In part, the "women problem" may have served as a welcome diversion from the need to reflect on the lessons of Vietnam and the difficulties of maintaining a volunteer, peacetime military with an ambiguous mission. Indeed, women may have been just the right problem—not too large, not too serious—and, in addition, they were new, they rarely made demands, and their congressional and other allies lacked sustained, intense interest.

Reforming the Military

The solution to the problem, it was often implied, was to get rid of the women. If the goal had been to make women accepted, effective participants in the nation's defense, there are a number of things the military could have done differently, even without removing the chronically irritating combat restriction. First, incentives for enlistment and reenlistment could have included guaranteed day care and joint-spouse assignment. These inducements would be no more "unfair" than currently offered reenlistment bonuses, educational benefits, and guaranteed geographic assignments, even if they did prove more attractive to women than to men.

Second, promotion criteria could be changed to accommodate specialized careers (for both men and women). Third, equipment could be redesigned for easier use by women (and smaller men). Fourth, the military could acknowledge that current "sex-blind" or "gender-free" policies are an experiment and inaugurate a new program of experimentation in which the differing effects of all-female units, all-female MOSs [military occupational specialties], and 50-50 units would be explored. Speculation would be fruitful, too. What if women were given the Air Force and the other three services were left to men? What if women were given all repair jobs or all supply jobs or all communications jobs?

Fifth, the military's role as a social institution should be recognized, and just as young men are trained and prepared for work in civilian life, young women could be supported as mothers. How to support the successful pregnancies of short-term, unskilled workers is a grave problem for the nation and all employers. A general solution is required—the military cannot be exempt.

Sixth, many of the jobs open to women should probably be reserved for them. This position assumes that the military would benefit from enlisting young people in a ratio approaching their availability. Thus, if men are required for one-third of a service's jobs, two-thirds of the remaining two-thirds could be earmarked for women, giving them slightly less than half of all jobs.

Seventh, the services could give more attention to learning what builds women's morale, what welds women and men into a cohesive team, what is required to lead women, and what is needed to teach men to respect and follow women's leadership. (The need to reintegrate basic training seems almost self-evident.)

The Male View

Much research on military women has been directed toward presumed deficiencies: attrition, job migration, pregnancy, single parents, and military couples. Moreover, much has been made of the "opening" of a handful of jobs in a few new fields, while dubious physical standards and equipment design that disqualify thousands of women are ignored. (The Air Force is not the only service that attempts to get the attentive, critical audience to focus on gnats rather than camels.) . . .

General Vessey should be taken seriously. The military is a male institution, and unless its very nature changes, women will continue to be indigestible. This will be especially true so long as it is possible to pretend that women can be excluded from combat.

Judith Hicks Stiehm is provost of Florida International University in Miami. She is also the author of Bring Me Men and Women: Mandated Change at the U.S. Air Force Academy.

"Sending American women out to fight and to try to kill enemy men is contrary to all historical experience, common sense, and the American culture."

The Military Should Employ Fewer Women

Phyllis Schlafly

The same week that Middle East terrorists and the hostage problem dominated the news, the *New York Times* featured a front-page story headlined "West Point Picks Woman to Lead Cadet Corps." The position of first captain of the Corps of Cadets, the academy's highest honor, puts her in charge of overseeing virtually all aspects of life for the 4,400 West Point cadets.

The picture showed a casual, T-shirted, straggly-haired 20-year-old girl. What do you suppose the bad guys of the world—the terrorists, the Soviets, the Chinese thugs, Qaddafi or Castro—think when they see this image of the one selected to lead West Point seniors?

West Point's Superintendent, General Dave R. Palmer, said, "She does not have the position because she's a woman." He is correct, but not the way he meant it. She has this honor because he is a wimp who toadies to the feminists who are constantly breathing down his neck and demanding more "career opportunities."

The *Times* article tried to reassure its readers that she deserves this position of leadership over all other West Point cadets, 90 percent of whom are men, by saying she has "a strong academic record, played soccer and competed in cross-country skiing." And one more qualification: she "worked as a speechwriter in the Pentagon." As Queen Victoria would have said, "We are not amused."

The Superintendent who made this newsworthy choice must think his mission is to train young people to be paperpushers in the Pentagon in a peacetime military, while keeping fit with athletics (but not the really tough men's sports). But if that's all West Pointers are being trained for, the cadets can go to any state university at one twentieth the cost to the taxpayers.

When General Douglas MacArthur, hero of three wars and the most distinguished cadet who ever graduated from West Point, delivered his great "Duty, Honor, Country" commencement speech there on May 12, 1962, he gave it to them straight. "Your mission remains fixed, determined, inviolable. It is to win our wars. Everything else in your professional career is but corollary to this vital dedication. . . . You are the ones who are trained to fight."

MacArthur continued, "Yours is the profession of arms, the will to win, the sure knowledge that in war there is no substitute for victory, that if you lose, the Nation will be destroyed." Times and weapons have changed, but the mission of West Point graduates is—or should be—the same as it ever was.

The Feminization of the Military

This is not a mission for girls (even if they excel in skiing and speech-writing), but a mission for real men. As MacArthur said, West Point must graduate men who, whether they are "slogging ankle deep through mire of shell-pocked roads, . . . blue-lipped, covered with sludge and mud, chilled by the wind and rain," or, on the other side of the globe, in "the filth of dirty foxholes, the stench of ghostly trenches, the slime of dripping dugouts," in "the loneliness and utter desolation of jungle trails," can be relied on to muster the strength and courage to kill the enemy.

Can we believe that this 112-pound, 5-foot-4-inch girl can do that—and, in addition, lead troops of men to risk death under such circumstances? You have to be kidding!

The official excuse for this catering to the feminists is that the baby boomers are now past military age, causing a shortfall of men who will volunteer for the All-Volunteer Force. But the real reason why there is a shortfall of male volunteers is not demographics; it is the feminization of the military.

Men are attracted to serve in the military because of its intensely masculine character. The qualities that

Phyllis Schlafly, "The Feminization of the U.S. Military," *The Phyllis Schlafly Report,* September 1989. Reprinted with permission.

make them courageous soldiers—aggressiveness, risk-taking, and enjoyment of body-contact competition—are conspicuously absent in women.

Fighting wars is a mission that requires tough, tenacious and courageous men to endure the most primitive and uncivilized circumstances and pain in order to survive in combat against enemies who are just as tough, tenacious and courageous, and probably vicious and sadistic, too. The armies and navies of every potential enemy are exclusively male and no women diminish their combat readiness.

Pretending that women can perform equally with men in tasks that require those attributes is not only dishonest; it corrupts the system. It discourages men from enlisting and it demoralizes servicemen from developing those skills that produce Douglas MacArthurs and George Pattons in our country's hour of need.

The Military Double Standard

If you want to know how America sank to this ridiculous situation, you should read Brian Mitchell's book called *Weak Link: The Feminization of the American Military* (Washington, D.C., Regnery Gateway, 1989). It's the definitive book on how the radical feminists have caused our military officers to cower in fear and to acquiesce in policies that make the integration of females a higher priority than combat readiness.

Mitchell, who served seven years as an infantry officer and is now a reporter for *Navy Times* newspaper, chronicles how this happened and documents the profoundly disruptive effect which women have had (such as ten percent of them being pregnant at any one time). Our top active-duty officers have bugled retreat on this issue and surrendered to feminist ideology and androgynous experimentation.

"Pregnancy is a constant problem and a reminder of the gender differences between men and women. In the course of a year, 10 to 17 percent of all servicewomen are pregnant."

The service newspaper *Army Times* editorialized: "Mitchell has dared to utter every male soldier's darkest doubt: that the American Army will come apart when women start dying in battle." Mitchell's book is must reading for anyone who cares about the national security of the United States.

There is no real evidence that technology has reduced the need for physical strength among military men. Evidence shows that most military jobs still require more physical strength than most women possess. The result is that the males in the services do more work to make up for the shortcomings of their female co-workers.

Mitchell says, "All of the services have double standards for men and women on all the events of their regular physical fitness tests. Young male marines must perform at least 3 pull-ups to pass the test, but women marines must only hang from the bar with arms flexed for 16 seconds. In the Army, the youngest women are given an extra three minutes to complete a two-mile run. All of the services require men to perform more situps than women, despite their much-vaunted strength of the female midsection."

A Weak Army

Mitchell shows that the rifles and pistols selected by the Army are not the best but those that are lighter-weight and more comfortable for women to handle. He concludes, "American soldiers are unlikely to get the weapon they need if it makes life more difficult for women."

George Washington instructed his officers: "Discipline is the soul of the Army. It makes small numbers formidable; procures success to the weak, and esteem to all." But discipline is out of fashion in a military that bends the rules to be nice to women, to accommodate their lesser physical strength and pregnancies and baby-tending, and to wink at fraternization and promiscuity.

Mitchell explains, "The presence of women inhibits male bonding, corrupts allegiance to the hierarchy, and diminishes the desire of men to compete for anything but the attentions of women." The romantic and sexual relationships between individual men and women defy regulation and dramatically affect the daily work relations of men and women.

Attrition rates (the failure to complete an enlistment contract) are consistently higher for women than men. A high attrition rate reduces service strength, increases personnel disturbance, and makes maintaining the armed services more costly because it cheats the taxpayers out of their investment in training. Women in all the services are hospitalized two to three times as often as men.

Pregnancy is a constant problem and a reminder of the gender differences between men and women. In the course of a year, 10 to 17 percent of all servicewomen are pregnant. At any one time, 5 to 10 percent are pregnant, and some small units have at times reported pregnancy rates as high as 50 percent. Servicewomen are eight times more likely to be single parents than men. If a pregnant soldier resigns, she contributes to the problem of attrition (but still gets maternity care until six weeks after delivery), and if she keeps her baby she contributes to the growing demand that the military provide daycare. Either way, she is a burden to her unit because a pregnant woman or recent mother is exempted from so many duties while her male co-workers must pick up the slack. The military is now one of the largest daycare providers, and is currently asking Congress for money for 81,000 more daycare slots.

Look at the 1989 case of 21-year-old Spc. 4 Cheryl Beekman who had a baby when she still had a year and a half left to serve of the term for which she had enlisted. Under Army policy, a pregnant soldier gets full maternity coverage and is also given the choice of an immediate release or signing a statement that after the baby is born she will accept whatever assignment comes down for her and her unit. Beekman chose the latter option and received all the special treatment the Army gives, including limited duty during pregnancy and 42 days leave after the baby was born followed by limited duty for six months with no strenuous tasks. Then the orders came for her to be transferred to South Korea and she didn't want to go. Surprise, surprise! Beekman hired a lawyer and filed suit, and the Army caved in like a deck of cards and let her out of her signed contract.

The Cover-Up and Deception

Our military men know exactly how to develop tough, trained soldiers who can win our country's wars. The historical record is clear. They also know, as Vietnam veteran James H. Webb, Jr. so eloquently wrote in his famous *Washingtonian* magazine article, that "Women Can't Fight" (November 1979). But the official line in the military and on the media is that women soldiers are performing just as well as men.

The performance record of women in the American military is the biggest cover-up in twentieth century politics and the greatest military deception carried out in modern times. Brian Mitchell's book *Weak Link* is "an account of the creation of a lie." He wrote it "on behalf of the many thousands of military men who know the truth but are under orders not to notice that the Emperor has no clothes."

Mitchell sets forth the convoluted and contorted semantics the military uses in order to conceal the fact that women do not meet the same standards, take the same training, pass the same tests, or endure the same trials and discomforts as men. The officers refer to "dual standards" as a euphemism for double standards. They talk about "equivalent training" when it is self-evident it is not equal training. When commissions, awards, honors, and badges are passed out, everyone knows the women have not met the same requirements, but no one is permitted to say this out loud.

The military carries on systematic brainwashing to promote the notion that women must be fully integrated and promoted in all aspects of the services. Male soldiers are forced to close their eyes and their mouths both to women's failure to perform equally and to the preferential treatment given to women.

Mitchell explains the process like this: "Official publications of the services are filled with propaganda promoting a favorable view of servicewomen. Commanders are required to publicly endorse and enforce equal opportunity in the military. Units are assigned equal opportunity officers to watch over the climate of relations between the sexes and report violations of policy, much in the way the Soviet military has Communist Party officers assigned to units to keep commanders politically straight. Personnel are required to attend equal opportunity training, during which EO officers preach the sanctity of sexual equality and the folly and immorality of belief in traditional sex roles. The definition of sexual harassment has expanded to include the open expression of opposition to women in the military. Officers and senior enlisteds are kept in check by their performance reports." A bad mark can mean a career is derailed.

The Feminist Agenda

Twice a year the feminist thought-control brigade, called DACOWITS (Defense Advisory Committee on Women in the Services), meets to oversee female affirmative action in the military and to complain about the lack of "progress." They lobby shamelessly to promote women over men and to eliminate the laws and regulations that prohibit assigning women to combat duty. They lay a guilt trip on military officers and Defense Department officials because they haven't turned over fifty percent of the high-ranking jobs to women.

"The American taxpayers do not spend billions of dollars to maintain the U.S. Armed Services and military academies so that young men and women can enjoy 'upward mobility.' "

Federal law specifically excludes women from combat jobs, and Congress stoutly rejected a determined effort by President Jimmy Carter and the feminists in 1979 to repeal this prohibition. Carter's Secretary of the Army, Clifford Alexander, violated the spirit if not the letter of the law by redefining "combat" so narrowly that many Army women were assigned to positions formerly considered combat jobs. This policy of renaming combat jobs as "combat support" jobs, and then assigning women to them, has continued ever since.

To put a veneer of plausibility on this duplicitous policy, feminist agitators and the media have deliberately propagated the myth that women in the Israeli army are treated just like men. The fact is, as Mitchell says, that members of the women's component in the military, called Chen (which means charm), are barred from jobs involving physical strain, adverse environmental conditions, or combat. They serve as clerks, typists, nurses, teachers, and social workers, but definitely not as pilots, sailors, truck drivers, or combat infantrymen.

Mitchell concludes that "The American military has been used by a political faction with no concern for national defense—for no other purpose than to advance feminism. . . . So long as the military remains mostly male, the hounding of the services will never cease. To expect feminists to settle for less is to gravely mistake both their will and their intent."

Mitchell has accurately figured out that the goal of the feminists is a gender-neutral society. The cutting edge of this objective is the U.S. Armed Services, whose mission, traditions, and training all combine to build the stereotype of manliness, toughness in the face of adversity and pain, and physical strength to overcome the odds in all emergencies. That is what the feminists want to reduce to gender neutrality.

So Mitchell is correct when he predicts, "Feminists can be expected to oppose a return to the draft until the combat exclusion laws are struck down by the courts. When the legal basis for excluding women from the draft no longer exists, feminists are likely to support the draft as a means of forcing more American women into nontraditional lifestyles." Indeed, in the 1981 U.S. Supreme Court case of *Rostker v. Goldberg*, which upheld the male-only draft, the National Organization for Women filed a brief which alleged that exempting women from the draft and from combat roles consigns women to a "second-class status" and deprives women of "politically maturing experiences."

The Folly of Women in Combat

The American taxpayers do not spend billions of dollars to maintain the U.S. Armed Services and military academies so that young men and women can enjoy "upward mobility" or opportunities for education, travel and training in job skills.

The armies of all potential enemies are almost exclusively male. No other nation in the world has such a high percentage of women in the military as the United States. The Soviet Union's 4.4-million-member armed force includes only 10,000 women, and they do mostly clerical and medical work. Sending American women out to fight and to try to kill enemy men is contrary to all historical experience, common sense, and the American culture.

If there is any subject on which this poor planet earth has plenty of experience, it is fighting wars. The lessons of hundreds of wars speak with a thunderous voice that wars can best be won by trained, disciplined, healthy, vigorous, risk-taking young men. Why this is so was persuasively explained in an excellent article called "No Right to Fight" by Lieutenant Niel L. Golightly, U.S. Navy (*U.S. Naval Institute Proceedings*, December 1987), in which he also points out that virtually none of the advocates of women in combat have any combat experience.

There is no evidence in all history for the proposition that coed combat assignments in armies and navies will promote national security, improve combat readiness, or win wars. Even Hitler and the Japanese, when they ran short of manpower, found it more efficient to use underage and overage men in combat than female troops. Of the thousands of books written about World War II no one ever wrote that Hitler or the Japanese could have solved their manpower shortage problem by using women in combat.

"Ask any real man who has personally experienced combat if he wants his daughter assigned to combat."

The only two nations that used women in combat in modern times, the Soviet Union and Israel, have both abandoned the policy because it doesn't work. We should study their experience and find out why.

American women served honorably during World War II in separate services such as the WACS and the WAVES, and they could do so again today. It is the sex integration of males and females, and the pretense that they can perform equally, which is destructive of combat readiness, discipline, and morale.

The desire of military women for combat is in inverse relation to their rank. That is, the female officers seek their "career advancement" to be promoted to high rank and pay in the peacetime army, but female privates are certainly not demanding assignment to the combat infantry.

Between 1948 and 1969, the percentage of women in the military, even including nurses, never exceeded 1.5 percent and averaged 1.2 percent of the total active strength. Women never came close to reaching the 2 percent limit set by the law. Congress lifted the 2 percent ban in 1967, but women did not reach 2 percent until five years later, after U.S. troops were pulled out of Vietnam.

The most insensitive people in the nation today are the female officers who agitate for repeal of the laws excluding women from combat—knowing full well that the enlisted women who lack a college education would suffer the brunt of a change in the combat policy. Perhaps these female officers are dreaming of an army in which women officers would hold the command positions, while men would do all the dangerous, dirty, often-fatal combat jobs that are assigned to enlisted personnel.

Not an Equal Opportunity

The Armed Services should not be used as a social experiment in equal employment opportunity. Affirmative action for women in the military is just as ridiculous as it would be to make the Armed Services subject to the new "Disabilities Act," which requires detailed and costly practices in order to bring into the mainstream of employment and public accommodations all persons with every kind of handicap from paraplegia to alcoholism and dementia.

But, some agitators argue, don't women have just as much right to die for their country as men? Dying for your country is not the purpose of the Armed Services; their mission is to make enemy troops die for their country, and men are demonstrably better at that task than women. Ask any real man who has personally experienced combat if he wants his daughter assigned to combat.

If the men in the U.S. Armed Services are too wimpish to stand up to the foolish feminists and their unnatural demands, how can we count on our Armed Services to stand up to the Russians?

Phyllis Schlafly is a leading conservative activist. This viewpoint was taken from her newsletter The Phyllis Schlafly Report.

Women Should Be Tested in Combat

The New Republic

During the U.S. invasion of Panama, a female soldier who had been driving a truck for hours, ferrying troops into a combat zone amid sporadic enemy fire, was about to be pressed back into service when she started crying. Another woman, who had been performing the same job, approached her and, by some accounts, started crying too. Both were relieved of their duties—whether at their request or not remains unclear. After news of the incident reached the press, the Army took pains to convey that the women had not disobeyed orders or been derelict in their duty. On the contrary, according to an Army official quoted in the *Washington Post*, "They performed superbly."

There are a number of sympathetic and truthful things you can say about these two women. You can note that they exhibited an acute understanding of the dangers they faced, or that their behavior was no different from that of countless male soldiers who have been traumatized by war. But to call the overall performance of a soldier who breaks down and cries during combat "superb" is ludicrous, and patronizing.

This utterance embodies a particular form of disingenuousness that has clouded the debate over opening combat positions to women. Within the Pentagon there is deep opposition to the idea, but it almost never gets honestly expressed. High-ranking officers may, over a beer, list half a dozen things that scare them about a fully integrated military—one of which is that women might start crying during war. But when Pentagon officials are publicly asked about the issue, they generally shy away from honest doubts. And proponents of full integration seem no more eager for a thorough airing of possible pitfalls. Their working assumption is that the only real sources of opposition are sexism and the political cowardice of legislators who don't want to be seen as sending women to war.

The shallowness of the resulting debate is by itself a good argument for proceeding with Representative Pat Schroeder's plan to open some Army units in every type of combat specialty to women on a four-year test basis. Mere public discussion of the issue, it seems, is not going to get us very far.

Puzzling Logic

To the extent that the exclusion of females from combat roles has a stated rationale, it is that women should not be put at risk of physical harm. Even a position classified as non-combat may, under current policy, be closed to women if, in the event of war, it would be dangerous. The logic here is puzzling. Does a woman's life have greater moral value than a man's? Does a wounded woman suffer more than a wounded man? Neither question has a valid ring to it, and both are best left for contemplation by those women who want to go to war.

To further confuse things, this warped rationale for combat exclusion is half ignored in practice. Women are not allowed to fly fighter planes, but they are free to fly AWACS [airborne warning and control system] radar planes—which are so big, slow, and tactically important that they might as well have "Shoot me first" stenciled on their sides. Women can't fight in tanks, but they sit in communications trucks that may be in harm's way. They can't serve on destroyers, but they serve on supply ships that drop anchor alongside destroyers.

Individual paradoxes aside, the distinction between combat and non-combat jobs is, as Schroeder stresses, broadly eroding. In the era of cruise missiles and other "smart" weapons, front lines are not necessarily more vulnerable than rear supply lines. And in the Panama-style interventions that some see as the wave of the future, there is scarcely such a thing as a front line.

The only valid reason to keep women out of combat

"Soldier Boys, Soldier Girls," *The New Republic*, February 19, 1990. Reprinted by permission of THE NEW REPUBLIC, © 1990, The New Republic, Inc.

is if their presence is debilitating to what military types call the mission. This is a real possibility, but so far it hasn't been illuminated by much honest discussion. Opponents of the combat exclusion rule often act as if the only reasonable doubts about female soldiers have to do with physical strength and stamina. If so, of course, the solution is simple: women who pass all relevant physical tests can go to war. Thus a woman who can march, say, 30 miles with a 65-pound pack would be eligible for the infantry; a woman who can readily lift and load heavy artillery shells would be admitted to the field artillery. (Women are now permitted only in the longer-range "push-button" artillery, which fires, for example, Lance missiles.) The number of women passing relevant strength tests should grow over the years, as strength, in the increasingly technological military, declines in relevance.

Gender Differences

But strength and stamina are not the only pertinent biological differences between men and women. Men are, statistically speaking, more aggressive than women, and at least some of this difference is inherent—due to the effect of the male hormone testosterone on the brain. It is less clear whether other observed differences—in the propensity to take physical risks, for example—are also genetically based. But the aggression gap alone means that even if the military were gender-blind and physical strength were irrelevant, full parity would be highly unlikely; barring genetic engineering, there will never be as many women who want to kill, and are good at it, as men.

As with physical strength, differences between the sexes in aggressiveness or bravery needn't stand in the way of individual women; insufficiently aggressive women (and for that matter insufficiently aggressive men) can, in principle, be weeded out. This may be tricky. You can't tell how mean someone is by counting push-ups. There is no systematic effort to gauge such psychological factors in basic training, but some such tests may be useful adjuncts to the Schroeder plan.

"There is anecdotal evidence from Israeli military history that men are inclined to linger over a wounded female comrade, to the detriment of the larger mission."

The ultimate test of such tests, though, can only come in combat. If women who reach certain combat positions have a markedly higher rate of failure under fire, then they will have to be barred from those jobs. This may be unfair, but try telling that to the soldiers whose lives hang in the balance.

The second big issue that cannot be definitively settled without bloodshed is the effect of women on previously all-male groups. The hypothesis, advanced by some anthropologists and evolutionary biologists, that men are genetically predisposed to fight in groups remains controversial. It is unclear whether the intense bonds formed during war, and all the valor and sacrifice they inspire, result from "male-bonding" or simply "person-under-fire bonding." Either way, there is no doubt that introducing a woman into a previously all-male platoon will change the group dynamics (just as there is no doubt that comparably diluting a previously all-female group will change things).

One source of change, of course, is romance, along with any attendant distractions, rivalries, and conflicts of interest. Another possible problem is the patronizing of women; there is anecdotal evidence from Israeli military history that men are inclined to linger over a wounded female comrade, to the detriment of the larger mission. The list of other possible changes is long, but the question, in the end, is simple: After all the adjustments have been made, and the group has found some new equilibrium, will the change have been for the better, the worse, or neither? Perhaps some insight into this question can be gained in peacetime—through, for instance, mock combat between all-male units and integrated units. But the only way to find out for sure is amid live ammunition: open some Army combat units to women and wait for the next Panama. . . .

Too Little Combat Experience

Among the reasons for holding a real-war test of full military integration is that, surprisingly, there is little germane evidence on the modern historical record. The role of women in Israel's War of Independence has been exaggerated; of 4,000 Israeli soldiers killed, only 114 were women. (Still, it may be noteworthy that the most commonly cited reasons for Israel's subsequent combat exclusion rule were not any deficiencies on the part of female soldiers, but the frequency with which they were raped when captured and the already mentioned tendency of male soldiers to worry excessively about wounded women.) During World War II Soviet women fought the Germans and seem to have acquitted themselves ably, but accounts are sketchy. Moreover, the women fought in segregated units. The few NATO [North Atlantic Treaty Organization] armies that have opened all combat posts to women, such as Canada's and Denmark's, have managed to stay out of wars. (But the Canadian experience suggests that infantry is by far the hardest challenge for women; at last count, of 88 female infantry recruits, 78 had dropped out of basic training, and only one had graduated.)

The U.S. military has been fitfully heading toward full integration for nearly a century. The Army founded auxiliaries for nurses in 1901, and for decades thereafter kept women in what was deemed to be their place. They served in clerical posts during World War I; some were in the trenches as telephone operators, but not at the very front lines. In World War II the Army Air Corps used women as ferry pilots, flying radio operators, control tower specialists, and airplane mechanics, as well as stenographers and telephonists. Sixty-seven military nurses survived the horrors of Bataan and Corregidor and were held for three years in a Japanese prisoner-of-war camp. For the most part women were cordoned off in separate auxiliaries; their presence was thought temporary. WAVES, the acronym for the Navy's auxiliary, stood for "Women Accepted for Voluntary Emergency Service."

Postwar legislation sustained the women's auxiliaries, but it also put a ceiling on the number of female soldiers—only two percent of each service—and imposed the combat exclusion rule on the Navy and Air Force. (The Army's exclusion rule is Pentagon policy, modeled on the legislation.) The two percent ceiling was lifted in 1967, but only after Vietnam did the numbers rise to impressive levels—from under four percent in 1974 to more than eight percent by 1980.

Quality Service

It is probably not too much to say that women saved the post-Vietnam all-volunteer military, by making up for the critical shortage of "high quality" (i.e., competently educated) male enlistees during the 1970s. As the high unemployment rate of the early Reagan years enriched the pool of male recruits, efforts to recruit women slackened. But their numbers grew anyway, reaching nearly 11 percent in 1989, the highest of any NATO country.

West Point, like the other service academies, was integrated barely more than a decade ago. And this year the First Captain (the top-ranking cadet in the senior class) was a woman. Still, the zenith for women in the military, so far, was probably reached in Panama. The now-famous assault by Capt. Linda Bray's military police unit on the Panamanian guard-dog kennel was not, it turns out, quite as heroic or bloody as first advertised. But it appears to be the first time a woman has commanded a military unit in combat. And by all accounts she didn't bat an eyelash, much less shed a tear.

The New Republic *is a weekly journal of opinions about contemporary affairs published in Washington, D.C.*

viewpoint 25

Women Should Not Be Tested in Combat

Suzanne Fields and Joseph Sobran

Editor's note: The following viewpoint is in two parts. The first part was written by Suzanne Fields. The second part was written by Joseph Sobran.

I

We'll have to make arrangements for battlefield breast-feeding.

Absurd? Well, no more absurd than changing the law so that women must become combat soldiers.

Military maternity has to be a first consideration, because 10 to 15 percent of the women in the services are pregnant at any given time. Until 1978, women who became pregnant were subject to immediate discharge, but now they're allowed to remain in the military and are expected to return to duty six weeks after they give birth.

If they're called to surprise duty in the middle of the night and can't find a baby sitter, someone else has to be called up. (Wars won't wait.) Moms also have to move out of the barracks and off the ship, because, as the Navy concludes with an understatement the size of a fleet air arm—a barracks or a ship is "an environment unsuitable for care of a newborn."

Morning sickness, maternity checkups and child-care concerns create animosity in barracks and aboard ship, too, between service mates who have to shoulder extra duty and those who don't. But even as the services struggle to accommodate women's special needs, they're feeling pressure from feminists who want to fight, or at least want other women to fight.

The Panama Example

The new round of ammunition fired to abolish the exemption of women in combat was set off by Capt. Linda Bray, a Military Police officer who successfully led a team of men and women against a defended attack-dog kennel in Panama and showed herself to be the equal of many male commanders.

Capt. Bray deserves our appreciation. Suggesting that she sets an example for other women to train for combat loads her act of heroism with a symbolism it cannot carry. She did her job well, but Audie Murphy she was not.

Readiness, efficiency, preparedness are the essential ingredients for a trained army, and most women—nearly all women—at their very best fall far short of fighting standards. Training requirements at West Point, for example, have been lowered to make sure women have a fighting chance to qualify. The Defense Department estimates that female soldiers have only 55 percent of the muscle strength, only 67 percent of the physical endurance of men. That's a lot to lack.

Lower Standards for Women

Double standards for men and women are the norm on physical fitness tests. The Marines, for example, have learned that women can't do pull-ups like men, so they're asked only to hang from a bar with arms flexed for 16 seconds. The Army gives women an extra three minutes to finish a two-mile run.

Women in training for the Marines are excluded from grenade throwing because they can't throw it far enough to avoid killing themselves. When a federal court decreed that height and weight requirements for police candidates were discriminatory under Title VII, West Point eliminated height and weight requirements, too.

We're supposed to think now that the ability to fight isn't all that important in a soldier. "The whole combat thing has been a fiction," says Rep. Patricia Schroeder, Colorado Democrat, who will soon introduce legislation for equal opportunity in the military. "There is no such thing as a combat zone any more. One day a position can be in a combat zone, the next day it isn't."

Mrs. Schroeder, who has never seen combat, wants to require the Army to try a four-year trial program to allow women to prove themselves ready for combat. She does not say where the Defense Department will find the trial war.

"The only justification for war is to protect the feminine side of life, in which men themselves have their deepest stake."

Feminists arguing for women in combat make curious analogies. Women in male combat units, argue feminists on the editorial page of *The New York Times*, would cause no more distraction from the necessary soldier-to-soldier "bonding" than black soldiers did when they were introduced into white units. How odd to compare the sexual tension between male and female to the racial tension between black men and white men.

No Right to Be Soldiers

Once women couldn't be doctors, lawyers or Indian chiefs, argue other feminists, and now they're free to be all of the above. So why not combat soldiers? The short answer is that the military is not an equal opportunity employer. The business of armies is to be prepared to kill enemies, and the ability to kill is not something that most societies encourage women to learn.

When Betty Friedan visited West Point and met with women cadets, she was thrilled that they had not adopted false imitations of machismo. "Those rigorous exercises," she writes in *The Second Stage*, "the sheer use of all the aggressive energy they could muster against the physical and mockup military obstacles, might explain how positive, serene, almost tender they could feel toward their boy-soldier oppressors."

She was afraid the women might turn themselves into men. If women enter combat, that's exactly what they will have to do. In a real war, "serene" and "tender" only gets a soldier killed.

II

Now it can be told: Our combat troops in Panama included women. They were technically participating in support units, but some of them were actually engaged in heavy fighting. This contravenes the spirit if not the letter of U.S. law.

Rep. Patricia Schroeder, the Colorado Democrat renowned for her all-around silliness, is drafting legislation to make women in combat fully legal. It may not be an idea whose time has come, exactly, but is certainly an idea that was bound to occur to Mrs. Schroeder eventually.

Feminism has already made inroads into the U.S.

military, the damage and dangers of which are examined ruthlessly by Brian Mitchell in his book *Weak Link* (published by Regnery Gateway). Basically, he documents the intuition of any man who has arm-wrestled with a representative sampling of girls and women: Women are weaker than men, can't run as fast, and they get pregnant more often. At West Point they even score lower on written tests in military subjects, presumably because of a simple lack of interest.

Nobody except the doctrinaire supposes that the military would be improved by leading combat units with women. The problem is the doctrinaire, who are disproportionately powerful politically. Affirmative action has reached the military, forcing the abandonment of job-related testing that tends to filter out women. One typical result is that women are being assigned to roles they can't handle: They get assigned to artillery supply jobs when they are too weak to lift the shells. Mr. Mitchell shows how this pattern is repeated again and again, causing much wasted energy and demoralization. Furthermore, about 15 percent of the women in service are pregnant at this moment.

If having women in combat roles were a good idea in practical terms, as opposed to the terms of a peculiar ideology that happens to be current among us in 1990, it might possibly have occurred to Julius Caesar, Tamerlane and Napoleon, who were practical conquerors. But it has never occurred to any serious military thinker, unless you count Mrs. Schroeder in that category. In every known civilization, men have done nearly all the fighting.

Physically Inferior

Is this because women are physically inferior? Yes, of course. We shrink from using the word "inferior," no matter how accurate, because it has come to be construed as an insult in all circumstances. Yet we assume the inferiority of women when we segregate them competitively in athletics. If tennis were unisex, you'd never have heard of Chris, Martina and Steffi.

True, there is overlap between the sexes. The lady shot-putter may be more useful in combat than the neurasthenic male poet. Even so, most of us would rather see him than her at the front.

Why is this? Simply because the inferiority of women in certain departments does not mean that they lack human dignity. They have a dignity of their own, as women. They are not kept out of combat for the reason blacks used to be, namely, because they are held in contempt, but for the opposite reason: Our respect for them is not based on their relative competence in the masculine specialties.

Every society on Earth has felt that the distinction between the sexes is profound and primal. People even assign sexual traits to their divinities, though sophisticated theologies may tell them this is nonsense. Western civilization has reinforced sexual differentiation in various ways, as by trying to exempt women from the violence of war. This is not atavism but refinement.

The incidental inferiority of women to men in physical strength is as nothing compared with their beauty and fascination as the source of life and the carriers of our future. This is a difference for which the word "superiority" would be too feeble, because the difference is incommensurable.

Two Ways to Insult Women

There are two ways of insulting women. One is to treat them as mere conveniences for male pleasure. This is what feminists rightly object to. The other is to judge them by the same standards as men. This is what feminists insist on, except that they also want to exercise the feminine prerogative of waiving the rules for themselves.

The only justification for war is to protect the feminine side of life, in which men themselves have their deepest stake. It is absurd to expose women to it. The death or mutilation of a young man is a tragedy. That of a woman would be a horror beyond words—which may be why the Army was at first evasive about female casualties in Panama.

The best answer to Mrs. Schroeder would be an adaptation of an antiwar slogan of the '60s: Hell no, you won't go.

Suzanne Fields is a columnist for The Washington Times *and is nationally syndicated. Joseph Sobran is also a nationally syndicated columnist and a senior editor for* National Review.

bibliography

The following bibliography of books, periodicals,
and pamphlets is divided into chapter topics
for the reader's convenience.

Child Care

T. Barry Brazelton — *Families, Crisis, and Caring*. Reading, MA: Addison-Wesley, 1989.

Beth Brophy — "Corporate Nannies for a New Decade," *U.S. News & World Report*, December 25, 1989-January 1, 1990.

Margaret Carlson — "Catching Up on Child Care," *Time*, October 16, 1989.

Mona Charen — "Keep Socialism Out of Daycare," *Conservative Chronicle*, November 15, 1989. Available from *Conservative Chronicle*, PO Box 11297, Des Moines, IA, 50340-1297.

Congressional Digest — "Child Care: Pros and Cons," February 1990.

Lynn DeLapp — *More than Babysitting: Rethinking Child Care and Preschool Policies*. Sacramento, CA: Joint Publications Office, 1989.

Lorraine Dusky — "Mommy Tracks That Lead Somewhere Good," *Working Woman*, November 1989.

Maggie Gallagher — "Do Congressmen Have Mothers?" *National Review*, October 27, 1989.

Jessica Gress-Wright — "ABC and Me," *Commentary*, January 1990.

Staffan Herrstrom — "Sweden: Pro-Choice on Child Care," *New Perspectives Quarterly*, Winter 1990.

Patricia Horn — "Creating a Family Policy," *Dollars & Sense*, January/February 1990.

William F. Jasper — "My Mother the State," *The New American*, January 30, 1989.

Barbara Kantrowitz and Pat Wingert — "The Day Care Generation," *Newsweek*, Special Edition, Winter/Spring 1990.

James J. Kilpatrick — "Budget Can't Support Federal Child Care," *Conservative Chronicle*, November 15, 1989. Available from *Conservative Chronicle*, PO Box 11297, Des Moines, IA 50340-1297.

Phyllis La Farge — "A Day in Family Day Care," *Parents*, January 1990.

Tamar Lewin — "Small Tots, Big Biz," *The New York Times Magazine*, January 29, 1989.

Dorileen R. Loseke — "If Only My Mother Lived Down the Street," *Marriage and Family in a Changing Society*, edited by James M. Henslin. New York: Free Press, 1989.

J. Brian Phillips — "The Real Child Care Crisis," *The Freeman*, October 1989. Available from Foundation for Economic Education, Irvington-on-Hudson, NY 10533.

Virginia Postrel — "Who's Behind the Child Care Crisis?" *Reason*, June 1989.

Ronni Sandroff — "Helping Your Company Become Family-Friendly," *Working Woman*, November 1989.

Phyllis Schlafly — "Insolvable Problems of Federal Daycare." *The Phyllis Schlafly Report*, July 1989. Available from The Eagle Trust Fund, Box 618, Alton, IL 62002.

Julius Segal — "Honor Thy Children," *Parents*, December 1989.

Joseph P. Shapiro — "Staff Turnover May Be Day Care's Biggest Problem." *U.S. News & World Report*, October 23, 1989.

Mitsuko Shimomura — "Japan: Too Much Mommy-San," *New Perspectives Quarterly*, Winter 1990.

Tim Unsworth — "What the Church Has Taught About Child Care," *Salt*, November/December 1989. Available from *Salt*, 205 W. Monroe, Chicago, IL 60606.

Albert Wojnilower — "Declining Hegemony and Child Rearing," *New Perspectives Quarterly*, Winter 1990.

Alan Wolfe — "The Day-Care Dilemma: A Scandinavian Perspective," *The Public Interest*, Spring 1989.

Family

Joan Wester Anderson — "Mending Broken Family Ties," *McCall's*, January 1990.

Aimee Lee Ball — "Good-bye, Paycheck! Hello Apron!" *Mademoiselle*, January 1990.

Anne C. Bernstein — *Yours, Mine, and Ours: How Families Change When Remarried Parents Have a Child Together*. New York: Charles Scribner's Sons, 1989.

Lynda E. Boose and Betty S. Flowers — *Daughters and Fathers*. Baltimore: The Johns Hopkins University Press, 1989.

Bryce J. Christensen — "The Costly Retreat from Marriage," *The Saturday Evening Post*, January/February 1990.

Don Dinkemeyer and Gary D. McKay — "A Repair Manual for Fixing Relationships with Your Kids," *Fortune*, January 1, 1990.

James J. Drummey — "The War on Women," *The New American*, January 15, 1990.

James E. Ellis — "What Black Families Need to Make the Dream Come True," *Business Week*, January 22, 1990.

Jerrold K. Footlick	"What Happened to the Family?" *Newsweek, Special Edition*, Winter/Spring 1990.
Alan Gelb	"Alone Together," *Parents*, January 1990.
Lisa Grunwald	"Bringing Up Daddy," *Esquire*, November 1989.
James M. Henslin, ed.	*Marriage and Family in a Changing Society.* New York: Free Press, 1989.
Barbara Kantrowitz and Pat Wingert	"Step by Step," *Newsweek, Special Edition*, Winter/Spring 1990.
Ronald D. Kelly	"Building Strong Marriages," *The Plain Truth*, April 1990. Available from the Worldwide Church of God, 300 W. Green St., Pasadena, CA 91123.
Debra Kent	"The Daddy Trap," *Mademoiselle*, December 1989.
Ladies' Home Journal	"Stay-at-Home Moms Speak Out," November 1989.
John and Susan Vollmer Midgley	"Young Couples in the Church," *The Catholic World*, March/April 1990. Available from Paulist Press, 997 Macarthur Blvd., Mahwah, NJ 07430.
Daniel Morris	"Do Catholic Couples View Having Kids as a Given?" *U.S. Catholic,* May 1989.
Ingrid Nelson	"Fostering New Hope," *New Choices for the Best Years*, January 1990. Available from *New Choices for the Best Years*, PO Box 1945, Marion, OH 43305-1945.
Susan Moller Okin	"Change the Family; Change the World," *Utne Reader*, March/April 1990.
William J. O'Malley	"Parents Are Apostles," *America*, January 20, 1990.
Brian O'Reilly	"Why Grade 'A' Execs Get an 'F' as Parents," *Fortune*, January 1, 1990.
Andrew Patner	"Shifting Suburbs," *The Wall Street Journal*, March 9, 1990.
Ollie Pocs	*Our Intimate Relationships: Marriage and the Family.* New York: Harper & Row, 1989.
William Sayres	"Parenting: The Best of Times or the Worst of Times?" *The World & I,* September 1989.
William Sayres	"What Is a Family Anyway?" *The World & I,* September 1989.
Jim Schachter	"The Daddy Track," *Los Angeles Times Magazine*, October 1, 1989.
Jean Seligmann	"Variations on a Theme," *Newsweek, Special Edition*, Winter/Spring 1990.
Arlene S. Skolnick and Jerome H. Skolnick, eds.	*Family in Transition: Rethinking Marriage, Sexuality, Child Rearing, and Family Organization.* Glenview, IL: Scott, Foresman, 1989.
Gary Sledge	"The Woman in the Kitchen," *Reader's Digest*, September 1989.
Anthony Walton	"The World According to Claude," *Reader's Digest*, January 1990.

Religion

Barbara Bartocci	"God, My Mother, and the Catholic Church," *St. Anthony Messenger*, July 1989. Available from *St. Anthony Messenger*, 1615 Republic St., Cincinnati, OH 45210.
Joan Carlson Brown and Carole R. Bohn, eds.	*Christianity, Patriarchy, and Abuse.* New York: Pilgrim Press, 1989.

Robert E. Burns	"The Church Shouldn't Believe in Never-Never Land, *U.S. Catholic*, February 1990.
Rita-Lou Clarke	"The Bible and Battered Women," *Daughters of Sarah*, May/June 1989. Available from *Daughters of Sarah*, 3801 N. Keeler, Chicago, IL 60641.
William Cleary	"Sex Achieved a Lot for This Priest," *National Catholic Reporter*, November 24, 1989.
Nancy Cross	"A Traditionalist's Dilemma: What to Do When the Pope Goes Feminist?" *Crisis*, January 1990.
Nadine Foley	"The Nature of Religious Life," *Origins*, August 31, 1989.
Monica Furlong	"The Pope's Lost Battalions," *The Witness*, January 1989. Available from *The Witness*, PO Box 359, Ambler, PA 19002.
John Garvey	"Women's Ordination: Another Go at the Arguments," *Commonweal*, January 26, 1990.
Richard Gilsdorf	"Woman Among the Women," *The Mindszenty Report*, May 1989. Available from Cardinal Mindszenty Foundation, PO Box 11321, St. Louis, MO 63105.
Daniel A. Helminiak	"Doing Right by Women and the Trinity Too," *America*, February 11, 1989.
Carter Heyward	*Speaking of Christ: A Lesbian Feminist Voice.* New York: Pilgrim Press, 1989.
Carter Heyward	*Touching Our Strength: The Erotic as Power and the Love of God.* New York: Pilgrim Press, 1989.
Othmar Keel	"Yahwe as Mother Goddess," *Philosophy & Public Affairs*, Fall 1989. Available from The Johns Hopkins University Press, Journals Publishing Division, 701 W. 40th St., Suite 275, Baltimore, MD 21211-2190.
Karen Ludwig	"Womanist Theology/Feminist Theology: A Dialogue," *Daughters of Sarah*, March/April 1989. Available from *Daughters of Sarah*, 3801 N. Keeler, Chicago, IL 60641.
Michael McGough	"The Lefebvrite-Feminist Coalition," *The American Spectator*, August 1989.
Emmett P. O'Neill	"He Would Do It All Over Again and Take the Celibacy in Stride," *National Catholic Reporter*, May 19, 1989.
Richard N. Ostling	"Can A Priest Be a Husband?" *Time*, January 22, 1990.
Richard N. Ostling	"Episcopalians' Semi-Schism," *Time*, June 19, 1989.
Judith Plaskow	"'It Is Not in Heaven': Feminism and Religious Authority," *Tikkun*, March/April 1990.
Rosemary Radford Ruether	"Bury the Crucible, Shatter the Self-Inflicted Spell," *National Catholic Reporter*, March 17, 1989.
Richard S. Sisson	"New Opportunities, Many Questions," *Moody Monthly*, January 1990.
Time	"Priestless Rites," November 20, 1989.
Phyllis Tribe	"The Pilgrim Bible on a Feminist Journey," *Daughters of Sarah*, May/June 1989. Available from *Daughters of Sarah*, 3801 N. Keeler, Chicago, IL 60641.
U.S. Catholic	"Does God Want to Be Your Macho Man?" May 1989.

Christin Lore Weber	*Blessings: A Womanchrist Reflection on the Beatitudes*. San Francisco: Harper & Row, 1989.
The Witness	"Second Woman Bishop Elected," January 1990. Available from *The Witness*, PO Box 359, Ambler, PA 19002.
Kenneth L. Woodward	"Feminism and the Churches," *Newsweek*, February 13, 1989.
Gretchen E. Ziegenhals	"Digging in the Gardens of Feminist Theology," *The Christian Century*, March 8, 1989.

Women in the Military

Mike Blair	"Girls in Combat Argument Rages," *The Spotlight*, February 12, 1990. Available from *The Spotlight*, 300 Independence Ave. SE, Washington, DC 20003.
Peter Cary with Liz Galtney, Joannie M. Schrof, and Peter Ross Range	"Breaking Barriers in the Barracks," *U.S. News & World Report*, August 21, 1989.
Mona Charen	"Women in Combat Is Absurd," *The Conservative Chronicle*, January 24, 1990. Available from *Conservative Chronicle*, Box 11297, Des Moines, IA 50340-1297.
Marlene Cimons	"Women in Combat: Panama Stirs Debate," *Los Angeles Times*, January 11, 1990.
Helen M. Cooper, Adrienne Auslander Munich, and Susan Merrill Squier	*Arms and the Woman: War, Gender, and Literary Representation*. Chapel Hill: University of North Carolina Press, 1989.
Peter Copeland	"Army Women Went into Panama with Weapons—and Used Them," *The Washington Times*, January 2, 1990. Available from *The Washington Times*, 3600 New York Ave. NE, Washington, DC 20002.
Marilyn Gardner	"Bearing Arms—Now a Woman's Question," *The Christian Science Monitor*, November 16, 1990.
Richard D. Hooker	"Affirmative Action and Combat Exclusion: Gender Roles in the U.S. Army," *Parameters*, December 1989. Available from Superintendent of Documents, U.S. GPO, Washington, DC 20402.
Los Angeles Times	"What if Mom *Does* Wear Combat Boots?" January 11, 1990.
Brian Mitchell	*Weak Link: The Feminization of the American Military*. Washington, DC: Regnery Gateway, 1989.
Molly Moore	"Can They Be All That They Can Be? Despite Their Numbers, Women in the Military Are Still Struggling," *The Washington Post National Weekly Edition*, October 2-8, 1989.
William Murchison	"Equal Opportunity Hits Army Where It Hurts," *Conservative Chronicle*, September 20, 1989. Available from *Conservative Chronicle*, Box 11297, Des Moines, IA 50340-1297.
William Murchison	"Rep. Pat Schroeder's Proposal Is a Turkey," *Conservative Chronicle*, January 31, 1990. Available from *Conservative Chronicle*, Box 11297, Des Moines, IA 50340-1297.

National Review	"Women in Battle," February 5, 1990.
Newsweek	"'No Slack': A Woman's Touch at West Point," August 21, 1989.
Phyllis Schlafly	"The Lesson of Women in Combat in Panama," *Conservative Chronicle*, February 7, 1990. Available from *Conservative Chronicle*, Box 11297, Des Moines, IA 50340-1297.
Mary Suh	"Canadian Women at Arms: Combat Duty Is No Longer a Male Preserve," *Ms.*, June 1989.
Time	"Fire When Ready, Ma'am," January 15, 1990.
U.S. News & World Report	"A Fresh Shot at Full Equality," January 15, 1990.
Christine L. Williams	*Engendering Difference: Women in the Marine Corps and Men in Nursing*. Berkeley: University of California Press, 1989.

Work

Joan Acker	*Doing Comparable Worth: Gender, Class, and Pay Equity*. Philadelphia: Temple University Press, 1989.
Jean Marie Angelo	"The World of Women M.D.'s," *East West*, April 1989.
Gloria Averbuch	"Doing the Double Juggle," *Ms.*, January/February 1989.
Barbara J. Berg	"Working Mother Overload," *Redbook*, March 1989.
Aaron Bernstein	"What's Dragging Productivity Down? Women's Low Wages," *Business Week*, November 27, 1989.
Beverly Beyette	"A Balancing of the Bar: Women in Law Find Profession Is Still in Favor of Men," *Los Angeles Times*, December 11, 1989.
Stephen Chapman	"Lawmakers Care Only for the Working Woman," *Conservative Chronicle*, February 7, 1990. Available from *Conservative Chronicle*, Box 11297, Des Moines, IA 50340-1297.
Alison Leigh Cowan	"Women's Gains on the Job: Not Without a Heavy Toll," *The New York Times*, August 21, 1989.
Pamela J. Creedon	*Women in Mass Communication*. Newbury Park, CA: Sage Publications, 1989.
E.J. Dionne Jr.	"Struggle for Work and Family Fueling Women's Movement," *The New York Times*, August 22, 1989.
Susan Eisenberg	"Women Hard Hats Speak Out," *The Nation*, September 18, 1989.
Bruce Fein	"Their Noble Cause Gone Mad," *The Washington Times*, October 31, 1989. Available from *The Washington Times*, 3600 New York Ave. NE, Washington, DC 20002.
Joanne Forman and Katherine H. Kleckner	"Women Workers Still Not Free," *New Unionist*, March 1989. Available from *New Unionist*, 621 W. Lake St., Suite 210, Minneapolis, MN 55408.
Marion Goldin	"Father Time: Who's on the Op-Ed Page?" *Mother Jones*, January 1990.
Blythe Hamer	"When the Boss Becomes Pregnant," *Psychology Today*, January/February 1989.
Susan Hartman	"Onetime Execs, Full-Time Moms," *The Christian Science Monitor*, September 25, 1989.

Arlie Hochschild with Anne Machung	*The Second Shift*. New York: Viking, 1989.
Karen Levine	"Are Dads Doing More?" *Parents*, June 1989.
David Machlowitz	"Corporate Moves: Achieving a Delicate Balance," *ABA Journal*, August 1989.
Margaret A. Palmer	"The Gender Gap in Science," *The World & I*, March 1989.
Fran Sussner Rodgers and Charles Rodgers	"Business and the Facts of Family Life," *Harvard Business Review*, November/December 1989.
Felice N. Schwartz	"Management Women and the New Facts of Life," *Harvard Business Review*, January/February 1989.
John Skow	"The Myth of Male Housework," *Time*, August 7, 1989.
Cindy Skrzycky	"Putting Employers on the Family Track," *The Washington Post National Weekly Edition*, September 11-17, 1989.
Elizabeth Spayd	"The Baby Broom: Juggling a Career and Family Tends to Sweep a Woman Off the Fast Track," *The Washington Post National Weekly Edition*, October 30-November 5, 1989.
Harry F. Waters and Janet Huck	"Networking Women," *Newsweek*, March 13, 1989.
Working Woman	"Are You Ready for the '90s?" January 1990.